BACHELOR STYLE

ARCHITECTURE & INTERIORS

BACHELOR STYLE

ARCHITECTURE & INTERIORS

THOMAS
DUNNE
BOOKS

ST. MARTIN'S PRESS

175 Fifth Avenue, New York, N.Y. 10010

Distributed in Canada by H. B. Fenn and Company, Ltd

PRINTED IN ITALY

Created by Co & Bear Productions (UK) Ltd.

Copyright © 2002 Co & Bear Productions (UK) Ltd.

Photographs © Various(2002). see p.216. Represented by Red Cover.

Text © Various(2002). see p.216. Represented by Red Cover.

ISBN 0-312-30399-8

Design by Coralie Bickford-Smith

Printed and bound in Italy,
at Officine Grafiche De Agostini.

First published in the United Kingdom by Scriptum Editions

First U.S. Edition

10 9 8 7 6 5 4 3 2 1

1:0 THE PLAYBOY

The playboy is undoubtedly the most modern of bachelor types. The very word implies a state of permanent bachelorhood – a 'boy' who lives to 'play'. Or, as the dictionary defines him, 'a man, especially a wealthy man, who sets out to enjoy himself'. Playboys are the least inclined to marry and settle down. Instead, they wring the very best out of their carefree existence. Unrestrained by tradition or by conventional social mores, they do as they please – more often than not in their playboy pads. Hugh Hefner and his Playboy Mansions may represent the vulgar side of the 'swinging' bachelor, but there are plenty of stylish playboys who know how to dress, decorate and entertain with panache.

For the modern man about town, the cosmopolitan connoisseurs Quentin Crisp and Donald Carroll give the following advice in their handbook *Doing It With Style*: 'If you are a person with style ... you will see your home as another medium for your message: something you put around you, like your clothes, in order to tell people who you are ... Needless to say, there is no such thing as a 'good address' or a 'bad address' where style is concerned. Style does not reside in any particular part of town. At the same time it is also true that people with style tend to avoid areas where all the semi-detached houses have names.'

Invariably, the playground of the playboy is the big city. With its restaurants and bars, its vibrant energy and its abundance of things to do, the city is the perfect playboy environment. Moreover, it is the ideal place for meeting people. The playboy's social life is all-important. For cultivating contacts, friends and lovers, the playboy relies on the metropolitan melting pot. For this same reason, the apartment is often the playboy's home of choice. It is easy to look after, and can be locked up and left in a hurry, should the playboy wish to jet off for the weekend at short notice. The modern apartment is light and airy, with sharp lines and masculine styling. It is clutter-free and open-plan, with emphasis on entertaining areas. The kitchen is usually minimal – naturally, just big enough for a bar and some state-of-the-art kitchen gadgetry, but not so large that it takes up valuable partying space.

An apartment can also offer great views and a terrace for entertaining. Its open layout is the ideal backdrop for contemporary furnishings. Curvaceous furniture, created primarily for lounging, highly tactile surfaces and intimate lighting often feature in the playboy's home environment. Whether apartment or house, the lineage of today's playboy bachelor pad can be traced back to the mid-twentieth century. The 1960s and 1970s were undoubtedly the playboy's heyday. Pursuing a life of freedom, independence and excitement, young men of means – inherited or earned – developed a stylish and distinctive lifestyle. They lived an urbane and hedonistic existence that was, and still is, much admired and emulated. In the Hollywood films of the day, the playboy pad was the ultimate in cool. Like the apartment of Frank Sinatra's swinging bachelor in *The Tender Trap*, it was designed first to impress, and second to seduce. To that end, entertaining was the primary function carried out in the bachelor playboy's realm – an extension of the hip bars and clubs he frequented. Consider this post-party note written by one aspiring playboy of the day to his Hungarian housemaid, Anna, as recreated by the writer Bill Safire in *Playboy* (1959):

My dear, dear Anna: Look around. What a horrible mess! But what a wonderful party. Would you believe this single room would hold 40 people? Dancing, laughing, singing, wildly carrying on? Oh, my head ... Oh, is this joint a shambles. To itemise:

1. Some of the unbroken glasses can be salvaged.

2. The bottom part of the stove will never be the same.

3. From the looks of the ash trays, I have a feeling some of my guests were cremated.

4. Nobody will ever be able to explain how that large, kidney-shaped stain got on the wall, but maybe we can hang a picture over it.

5. The pillows are mashed down from now 'til Doomsday, and no amount of plumping will ever bring them to life. Save them, maybe I can use them on the beach next summer.

6. Get a repairman up to do something about the pretzels in the phonograph ...

Such was the life of the martini-guzzling mid-century bachelor. To entertain (and seduce) with style, his home was filled with the hippest interior accessories: from shag-pile rugs for the bedroom, and bongos and bamboo stools for the jungle bar, to groovy hi-fi and lava lamps for the lounge.

The twenty-first-century playboy is usually far less contrived in taste than his mid-twentieth-century cousin. And today's playboy 'lairs' are likely to be designed with less obvious intentions in mind. The modern playboy home is laid-back, easy to maintain and fun to live in. And, most importantly, it never sacrifices anything to pleasure.

1:1 SALVAGED SPLENDOUR

Jonathan Reed represents a new breed of London-based design professionals who work and live in the same building. However, to work and live in one large space – on the same floor and in the same building – is something totally different. With his telltale panache, Jonathan has managed to pull it off. 'It all came about when I saw an unrenovated ... building in Chelsea,' he recalls. 'I had never seen such extraordinary proportions anywhere else in London, let alone Chelsea. I was hooked the moment I set eyes on the place.'

Built in the 1890s as one of a row of workhouses, the building was turned into a women's hospital shortly after World War II. It served temporarily as Chelsea Town Hall, and remained empty until a developer saw its potential a few years ago. 'I was able to get in quick and acquire one entire floor,' recalls Jonathan.

Jonathan set up Reed Creative Services in the mid-1990s. His company designs not only most of a client's furniture, but also the interior and architectural elements of a residence. He has a straightforward approach to everything he does and is fascinated by the simplicity of raw elements and natural materials. 'I also have a penchant for large-scale pieces,' he claims. His schemes are often discernible not just because of their content but by their scale, detail and the quality of the natural materials used.

Although originally designated for offices, Jonathan was able to acquire a lease that allowed him to split the floor into two separate units, providing him with discrete working and living areas. It is now neither a loft nor an apartment, and the living/dining/sleeping area is contained in one vast rectangular space. However, being in a preservation area, structural alterations were prohibited. The property was also leasehold, so Jonathan decided against investing too heavily in something he might not be living in for more than a few years. As is so often the case when there are strict budgetary restraints at work, the outcome shaped solutions that were entirely in keeping with the character of the building.

Take the steel columns and the vintage air conditioning, which under the lease could not be removed. Rather than try to conceal the somewhat primitive effects, Jonathan chose to emphasise them within the design scheme. As a result, the wiring is surface-mounted and the plumbing has barely changed; in fact, the bathroom is still where the doctors used to 'scrub up' before carrying out an operation. Downlighters were permissible where the ceilings had caved in – luckily, this was above the kitchen, where light is needed most.

'It's a very masculine space,' claims Jonathan. Indeed, two huge two-inch (5cm) thick mahogany doors signal the entrance between the flat and the office. A floating partition (less than two-thirds of the ceiling height) has been erected in the centre of the room, retaining a sense of unity and light. On one side of the wall is an open dining area with a circular bleached-oak table (one of Jonathan's designs), which is surrounded by chairs reclaimed from a sewing-machine factory.

To one side of the room a low screen made from American black walnut denotes the seating area (the other side faces the kitchen), where a large a four-seater 1970s leather sofa with side tables made of polished concrete blocks takes centre stage. Although Jonathan couldn't alter the space structurally, he modernised it with elements such as the brushed-steel fire surround, above which hangs a huge mirror set in a thick rusted metal frame.

The floor is almost entirely covered with a bordered carpet and the walls are painted a subtle shade of off-white. Khaki-coloured curtains and wooden Venetian blinds combine to provide shade from the midday sun, while a subtle colour palette incorporates shades of brown, tan, khaki and cream. The few accessories that do appear have been chosen with extreme care. 'I'm very disciplined and I know how to edit' admits Jonathan. The living area, with its drop-lights salvaged from a library, also houses a Japanese vase and a pair of 1960s ceramic lamps. The armless chair and Ottoman are Jonathan's designs.

The bedroom (on the other side of the central partition) has a run of three matching windows. A desk and a reading area have been arranged to one side of a large 1850s Burmese bed, while a plaster relief set in a simple square frame hangs above the fireplace. A pair of government-surplus filing cabinets have been painted and given new oak legs – demonstrating, again, Jonathan's passion for rescuing unusual items destined for salvage.

The kitchen (at the far end of the apartment) consists of a high wooden bar with a black corian top, under which a row of four metal bar stools are stored. On the other side of the bar is the work surface, which is also covered in corian. Although it's relatively small, it seems much more spacious because it's part of the overall space.'

The bathroom's slatted shelves, brushed-nickel taps and muted green tiles play up the handsome olive-green rubber matting to perfection. The room reflects the utilitarian feel of the building, using heavy-duty Belfast sinks instead of traditional basins.

The result is a triumph. Jonathan has managed to create a contemporary yet comfortable home. Last but certainly not least there's Bully, an Alsatian–bull terrier cross rescued from Battersea Dogs' Home. 'He's no doll,' says Jonathan with a smile. 'But ... the colour of his coat goes beautifully with the colour scheme.'

ABOVE & OPPOSITE The kitchen uses the same urban-commando-cool colour scheme as the rest of the flat. Both the high wooden bar and the lower-level cooking surface are covered in black corian. The cupboards are designed by Jonathan.

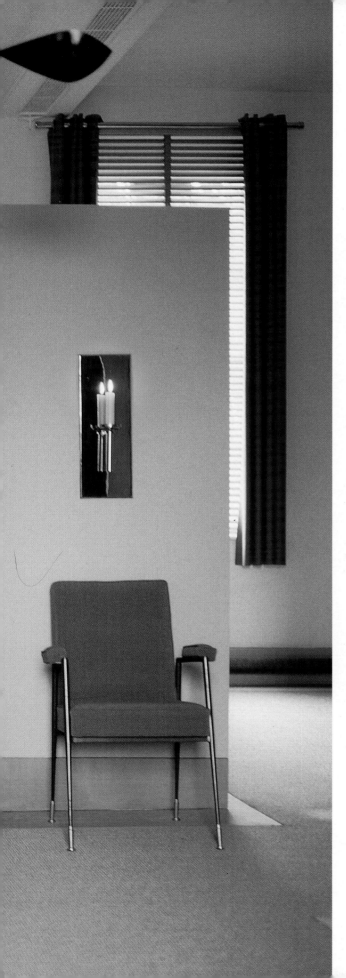

LEFT & ABOVE The French cabinet with woven pearwood doors is positioned along the floating partition of the open dining area. Both the cabinet and the two Leleu chairs that flank it are from the 1920s. Reed Creative designed the circular bleached-oak table and nickel sconces.

ABOVE & RIGHT Because structural changes to the flat were not permitted, Jonathan chose to make a feature of the original steel columns and heating system. The 1940s wing chair is covered in caramel coloured leather, and sits in front of one of the room's three fire surrounds.

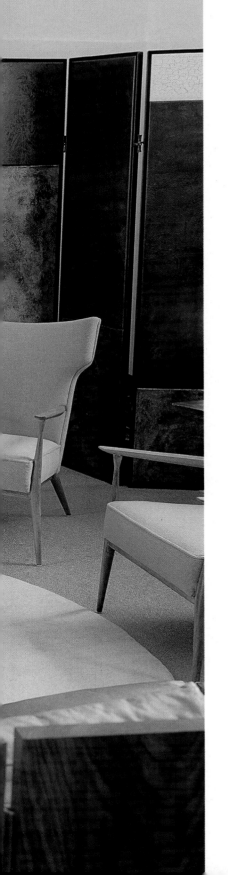

LEFT & ABOVE A low screen made from American black walnut denotes the seating area of the apartment, where the large 1970s leather sofa and polished concrete side tables take centre stage. A brushed-steel fire surround gives the area a more modern feel. The living area contains only a few carefully chosen accessories, such as this droplight salvaged from a Manchester library.

ABOVE & OPPOSITE   A 1940s red leather desk and black leather chair by Jacques Adnet create a reading area

beneath one of the apartments many windows. A heavy-duty Belfast sink, which fits in perfectly with the utilitarian feel of

the building, is a must for this room, which doubles up as a photographic darkroom.

LEFT & ABOVE   In the bedroom, two steel chests-of-drawers sit either side of a large 1850s Burmese bed. A plaster relief in a simple frame hangs above the fireplace with a brushed-steel surround, while to one side government-surplus filing cabinets have been painted green and given new oak legs.

ABOVE & RIGHT The bathroom's slatted shelves, brushed-nickel taps and green tiles play up the handsome olive-green rubber matting to perfection. Using heavy-duty Belfast sinks instead of traditional basins emphasises the size and scale of the building.

1:2 CITY RUSTIC

Tim Booth's ultimate fantasy is to live in a barn in the country – not unlike the converted one he grew up in. To date he hasn't yet fulfilled his dream, but he's come as close as he could have done in the big city. For five years, he's been living in a converted bakery in Brixton, south London, where he works as an Internet entrepreneur and travel photographer. Booth's living and working home also serves as the creative headquarters for his business. His Website, *www.iwantoneofthose.com,* sells outrageously luxurious, tongue-in-cheek goods that are close in spirit to Bond-movie gadgets. The Website has stocked ex-Russian Air Force fighter planes, a mini-blow torch cigarette lighter which (very niftily) can caramelise a *crème brûlée*, and remote-controlled UFOs that whizz round your home – presupposing, of course, that you live in one as cavernous as Booth's.

Given his talent for locating objects that fulfil people's wildest fantasies, it's not surprising Booth was able to track down his dream home. 'The moment I first walked through the door, I fell in love with it,' he recalls. He was looking for a home with original features that hadn't been tampered with or crassly gentrified. That said, he needed to make adjustments. 'It felt spartan and empty. Essentially, it was a shed not a house, but it had potential'. Still, any new additions clearly accord with the building's rugged aesthetic. In his bedroom, tucked behind the main living area, there's a rough-hewn sink, carved by a sculptor, while reclaimed wood from an architectural salvage company has been used extensively on floors, and even the kitchen work surface. Booth also installed a roof terrace – a separate structure specially suspended over the existing roof as the latter wasn't strong enough to take the weight of people tramping about on it. 'I love it. It's my little haven. I sleep up there on hot nights in summer'.

He thinks the building started life as a Methodist church, judging by its austere, rectangular shape. But vestiges of its past life point to the building's incarnation as a bakery – white tiles run along one wall where the ovens once stood, there's a mezzanine level once used to store flour (now a much-used TV room), and an old pulley that once hoisted up sacks of flour. The kitchen runs along one length of the living area, and was once the bakery's offices. Overlooking the living area, where Booth frequently throws dinner parties, are the original rafters, while his bedroom boasts plenty of exposed brickwork. He loves furniture and artefacts with a timeworn patina. Many of these have come from his travels round the world or were given to him by his grandfather (once a tea planter in Ceylon), a typical example being a horsehair fly swatter. Booth loves to improvise, recycling objects and finding new functions for them. An old cartwheel has been turned into a ceiling-hung candelabrum, an old first-aid box serves as a spice rack, and ancient organ pipes function as storage units.

ABOVE & OPPOSITE The kitchen runs along the length of the living area of the flat, and white tiles cover the wall where the ovens once stood. Tim loves to recycle objects and give them new functions – an old first-aid box becomes a spice rack, for example.

Which parts best reflect his personal style? 'The open beams and rough wood. The uneven surfaces, the place's organic feel. Above all, the wide, open spaces. If I were to create another home, suited to family rather than bachelor life, one thing I'd never compromise on ... would be having so much space – oh, and my large, lived-in kitchen.'

'I'm so fortunate to live in such an awesome place, that going out to a bar or pub isn't wildly appealing,' he continues. A self-confessed foodie, he loves having friends round for dinner. 'I do so as often as I can – my workaholic temperament permitting. I've a few musician friends who love playing here because the wall tiles create a great sound. Who needs the West End? Except for the theatre, of course!'

Although his job gives him the opportunity to globetrot, Booth confesses he's so enamoured of his home that he's a bit of a homebod. 'I love to flop in front of the TV and watch a truly terrible movie with a bottle of wine without feeling guilty.' The independence and privacy of his footloose bachelor lifestyle bring him many advantages: 'I can wander round at very unsociable hours thinking, playing music or working, without worrying about waking anyone up. The week rushes by in such a blur that I don't notice where I am, but at the weekend I can take time to appreciate my home. I can wake up on Saturday morning and potter around with power tools fixing things, read the paper, do the crossword, and not for a moment consider going shopping for anything but food. Often I'll do a big food shop and lose myself in the kitchen, cooking for a dinner party on a Saturday night.'

Although a new man, who feels as much at ease cooking as he does doing DIY, he concedes that his home contains what could traditionally be considered masculine features. 'My bedroom has a heavy, metal door which looks a bit like a prison cell door, but I love it because it's beautifully made. Then there's all the rough brickwork. There's not a lot of colour around, either – just the neutral tones of wood and brick.' But he feels uncomfortable about anyone pigeonholing his taste, and he's appalled by the idea that people can allow their taste to be dictated by anyone else. 'The end result is too self-conscious and tends to be overdone,' he winces. 'I'm anti-style, anti-designer labels. If you're going to design a place where you spend most of your time, it should be entirely to your taste.' Nothing, then, appears to constrain Booth's state of untrammelled independence. So, does his home life match the bachelor ideal of complete personal freedom? 'In every way, bar the presence of my cat, Rap, who's psychotically possessive!'

A human being who's more independent than a cat? Now that *must* be a first.

LEFT & ABOVE The bedroom, which is tucked behind the main living area, boasts plenty of exposed brickwork, and contains a rough-hewn sink carved by a sculptor. Reclaimed wood has been used extensively on the floors.

ABOVE & OPPOSITE Booth loves furniture and artefacts with a timeworn patina, many of which

have come from his world travels. The open beams, the rough wood and the place's organic feel

all reflect his personal style.

1:3 VERTICAL HARMONY

The Maison Vertical (Vertical House) is a three-storey living and workspace (or triplex) situated in Manhattan, New York. Designed by a six-person team at Marble Fairbanks Architects (MFA), led by co-partners Karen Fairbanks and Scott Marble, the residence is reminiscent of the *Maison de Verre* (House of Glass), a Parisian architectural classic from the 1920s. Like the *Maison de Verre*, the Maison Vertical, which is situated on Manhattan's West Side, uses glass and steel to establish an internal precinct of light-filled living and work spaces but within a tight urban site.

In *Modern Architecture Since 1900*, William J.R. Curtis describes the famous House of Glass, which was designed in Paris between 1928 and 1931 by Pierre Chareau and Bernard Bijopvet, as 'an elegant and translucent *machine à habiter* with a tranquil sense of place'. These same words could be used to describe the Maison Vertical, except that here the glass in question is transparent and appears on the floor rather than the walls. Close enough ...

'The project began as a simple stair connection between two apartments,' explains Karen Fairbanks. Next came the idea for a glass floor. This was introduced to bring natural light deep into the lower levels of the $14^{1/2}$-ft-wide town-house triplex. (It was previously divided up as a simplex on the third floor, and a duplex on the fourth and fifth floor, with a rooftop skylight.) From there, says Fairbanks, the scheme 'evolved out of specific needs that unfolded as the project proceeded. A change in one part of the apartment necessitated a change in another part.'

Complicated by the incremental nature of the project, the challenge for the architects was to work within the narrow confines of the town house and to solve programme relationships vertically. According to Fairbanks, 'the physicality of movement' became an organising force (like it was in the *Maison de Verre*), where retractable stairs are raised and lowered between floors and walls, and doors are opened and closed on tracks.

Movement through the triplex, which (including the roof terrace) measures 5000 sq ft, was guided by the client's living and work schedule. In contrast to the necessary separation of living and work spaces inside Dr Dalsace's Maison de Verre (the building was also used as medical clinic), the owner of the Maison Vertical requested that some rooms should be flexible enough to accommodate professional and private activities, with room functions changing as and when required. Hence, a conference and guest room occupies the third floor, along with an office; the fourth floor houses a living/conference/screening room, together with the kitchen and dining area; and the top floor, which is completely private, houses a gym and the master bedroom.

With a mandate to maximise the flow of natural light through the rooftop skylight, the team at Marble and Fairbanks designed a riser-free stair system that leaves the narrow light shaft open. Cantilevered from a steel tube buried in the party wall, triangular steel stairs with cast-rubber treads appear to be floating along one edge of the central light shaft. (The cantilevered steps, of course, do move slightly when they are being used.) Thanks to the dramatic but unobtrusive stairs and the 1in-thick glass floor which is set in a structural steel frame between the third and fourth storeys, the visual connection between the floors and their functions is cohesive.

The flexibility of the dual-purpose rooms also requires the visual – and sometimes physical – separation of one space from another by way of sliding walls and horizontal shades. The folding, sliding wall on the third floor, which is in fact a series of individual, layered plywood panels with a rubber laminate finish, opens and closes with a pull and push of the hand. A fabric shade, operated at the touch of a button, is mounted horizontally beneath the glass floor to separate the third storey from the floors above.

The kitchen can be closed off from the dining room with a similar fanfare. Even the client's 113kg (250lb) projector can be concealed within a drop ceiling in the fourth-floor living room by way of a computer-controlled lift. Yet another button lowers a screen across the living room's glass terrace doors.

The entire operation is all very Maison de Verre – very *machine à habiter*.

OPPOSITE & RIGHT The lowest level (third floor) of the residence has a home office and a conference room that converts into a guest room, via an ingenious sliding layered plywood door.

ABOVE & OPPOSITE   Natural light from a rooftop skylight above the middle section of the town house filters down three storeys,

straight through a 1in thick-glass floor. Open cantilevered stair treads mark the circulation route without blocking the distribution of light.

ABOVE & RIGHT The perforated sliding door (shown closed here) can be used in conjunction with horizontal shades under the glass floor and over the staircase, to separate work areas from the upper floors.

1:4 MODERN MOORING

When Charles Nicholson started looking for a new home, his first port of call was a flat in Wandsworth, on the River Thames. 'It was a newly built block with a gym and a swimming pool, which sounded rather nice,' he recalls. 'However, the developer had also installed a small marina directly in front of the building where he had a show flat in a boat moored to one of the pontoons.' Because of his own sailing background – his family owned Camper & Nicholson, the famous boatbuilders – Charles was captivated by the marina: 'It was an idyllic setup with unrivalled views in every direction ... I instinctively knew my next home would be right there on the water.'

He never did get to see the flat, and instead bought himself a 80ft boat. After two years of careful planning and hard labour, Charles is firmly ensconced in what he fondly terms his 'house on the river', a blue-and-white-painted, two-storey metal barge with every mod con imaginable (mains electricity, gas, water, sewage, central heating, cable TV, entry phone), plus garage and access to a swimming pool and gym.

Once bought, his first problem was where to store the barge during renovation. Luckily he found an unused draw dock in Fulham, where he was able to hook up to the electricity on a nearby building site. He then had to chop 6ft off the back of the barge, because it was longer than the contract stipulated. Just like with a house, it was important to get the structure right from the start. A new steel deck and roof was built over what was once the hold, and the entire boat was insulated, to prevent condensation. Next, a timber frame was erected inside the barge, but instead of using plasterboard Charles opted for MDF and tongue-and-groove panelling. Like most boat owners, his prime concern was fire. 'We put fire protection into the walls, and the brick hearth has a layer of sand, a steel frame and a further layer of asbestos just to be on the safe side.'

The overall layout now consists of a large deck house 50ft by 16ft, which contains the sitting room, kitchen and small cloakroom. From here, an unobtrusive staircase leads down to the master bedroom with en-suite bathroom and dressing room. A second set of stairs, at the far end of the kitchen, gives access to the study, spare bedrooms, and bathroom. Charles wanted to create a space that was light, open and practical. 'By introducing two sets of stairs I eliminated the need for a corridor, which would have restricted both space and light.'

The sitting room is light and modern, and decorated in off-white, cream and a strong shade of blue. 'The idea was to take full advantage of the view but to prevent people looking in, so we blanked off the wall facing the shore which in turn gave us somewhere to site the fireplace,' he explains.

At the top of the stairs in the sitting room stands an 8ft high scale model of a lighthouse with an original lighthouse light on the top, made specially for the room in a combination of woods. 'Although everything is built to the standard of a house, I wanted the occasional nod to the water,' admits Charles wryly.

A large opening at one end of the room leads into an airy kitchen where everything is overscaled and bold. Charles' sister Jane, an interior designer, helped with the layout and details. They chose white tongue-and-groove panelling for the walls in a design that is repeated in dark blue on the unit doors. 'My aim was to have a spacious, uncluttered kitchen,' explains Charles, which would explain the lack of wall units (indeed, both fridge and store cupboard are concealed behind large white tongue-and-groove doors, to blend in with the wall). A magnificent oak table, handmade by the carpenter, is surrounded by a set of chairs from Charles' new shop (he part-owns The Chair Company in Fulham).

Downstairs, the master bedroom and bathroom sit at the far end of the boat – away from the pontoon and prying eyes. Here, the decoration verges on minimal. As the windows were much smaller than those upstairs, light was a major concern. To create an impression of light, Charles panelled the room in MDF, painted off-white, and to emphasise the theme further the bed is boxed in with panelling and has a radiator concealed at the foot end.

A few steps from here lead up to the long and narrow bathroom at the very end of the boat. Because the bow is considerably higher than the rest of the boat, and runs the full width of the craft, it was difficult to create a conventionally shaped room. However, this made it perfect for concealing the plumbing. In keeping with the rest of the decoration, tongue-and-groove panelling offsets the shower at one end of the room and the basin at the other. The bath takes centre stage alongside a huge window overlooking Wandsworth Bridge and the city beyond. 'It's fantastic to lie in the bath and watch the world go by.'

His latest acquisition is a rubber inflatable boat with a diesel engine, which makes it perfect for the river. 'Depending on the tides we can go to the pub, the theatre, visit the Millennium Dome or shop at Sainsbury's, which is very convenient, apart from carrying the bags down the ladder – an extremely hazardous operation, especially in the dark.'

Charles' boat is not just a passing fancy; it is a home that is loved and cared for. In winter the barge is cosy and warm with a roaring fire, while in summer the doors are flung open and the barbecue set up on the deck. 'It's an incredibly civilised way of life. My neighbours are delightful and every so often we all get together for supper. It's a village on water.'

ABOVE & OPPOSITE There is a noticeable lack of wall units in the boat's bold and overscaled kitchen. White tongue-and-groove panelling was chosen for the walls, a design that is repeated in dark blue for the unit doors.

LEFT & ABOVE The sitting room is an oasis of calm, with panoramic views of the river – but is sheltered from the shore by the unsual addition of a fireplace. An 8ft scale model of a lighthouse with an original lighthouse light on the top, was made especially for the room.

ABOVE & OPPOSITE The light and modern sitting room is decorated in a palette of off-white, cream and blue. 'Although everything is built to the standard of a house, I wanted the occasional nod to the water,' the owner admits.

LEFT, CENTRE & ABOVE Light was a major concern in the bedroom so it has been panelled and painted in off-white. For the same reason, decoration has been kept to a minimum. The bed itself is panelled to match, with an ingeniously concealed radiator at one end.

1:5 ELEMENTAL ELEGANCE

It all began with a pressed-earth floor, a mysterious pool, a skylight and a crucible. Architect Patrizio Romano Paris's transformation of a former foundry in Rome is an ode to the four elements: 'I wanted to unite earth, water, air and fire in a single space,' he explains, as he leads the way down a long corridor into a large, light-filled room.

A mosaic-lined pool dominates the centre of the living area. 'This was inspired by the *impluvium*, the Classical rainwater pool found in the atrium of Roman houses,' the 53-year-old Renaissance man explains. 'As you can see, I love to combine the traditional with the minimalist and the modern.' And all this in a disused foundry built in the 1920s.

For anyone wanting to live and work in the same district, let alone in the same building, it's practically impossible to find an attractive residence in Rome. Unless you're prepared to live at one end of the Eternal City and work at the other, that is ... So when Patrizio chanced upon what was to become his new home, he didn't hesitate for a moment. 'I took only one look at the abandoned foundry next to the Botanical Garden, and I knew this was where I was going to live and work.' It took a year and a half to transform the run-down shell of an industrial building into a generously proportioned office on the one side and a unique, loft-like space on the other – incorporating industrial elements and designer furniture, the entire scheme guided by an unerring eye for the extraordinary.

Patrizio Romano Paris hankers after space rather than rooms, which is why – apart from the 1600 sq ft living room – the enormous space has only a bedroom, a kitchen and two bathrooms. 'I want to breathe, not stare at walls', he says with a smile. But before he could fill his lungs in the old foundry, it took 10 tonnes of iron to replace the dilapidated wooden roof with a modern construction supported by iron girders.

Patrizio had a marine inoko floor laid directly onto the pressed earth. He had already had plenty of opportunity to work with wood, which he appreciates not only for its beauty but also for its practicality. 'I'm a water rat and have sailed in regattas for years – even in the World Cup in Flensburg,' he adds with a modest smile. 'And besides my work as an architect I have been building boats for ages.' However, the floor isn't entirely covered in wood. In one corner, which has been left uncovered, rare species of palms from the Amazon rainforest grow straight out of the floor.

Anyone visiting the place will immediately recognise that water is Patrizio's element. Very few other people would have a heated swimming pool – measuring 23ft by 13ft, and fully equipped with massage jets – in the centre of their living room. What used to be the foundry's cooling basin is now where Patrizio chills out and relaxes: a black-and-white-tiled oasis of calm. The middle of the swimming pool is graced by a golden cube, and its shaded sides are represented in grey and dark green. This is a trompe l'oeil homage to minimalist artist Sol LeWitt, whose work Patrizio particularly admires.

In the way that he builds and lives, 'Less is more' is definitely Patrizio's motto. 'The more minimalist, the more convincing,' he explains. His love of graphically simple lines is also revealed in the striped mosaic-clad pillars, the square skylight and in the imposing fireplace, which is a perfect demonstration of his belief that building should be about 'keeping materials authentic'. The fireplace was made from the former crucible of the foundry – out of iron, of course.

'In a former life I must have lived in Japan,' says the native of Rome with a wink. 'Where else could my obsession for simplicity come from? Me of all people, a Roman in Rome?' But it is precisely Patrizio's pared-down aesthetic that makes him a highly sought-after architect and designer in this city of monumental, writhing, Baroque excess. No wonder the apartments he restores are just as extraordinarily original as the offices and private houses that he builds elsewhere in Italy, Monte Carlo or Greece.

Indeed, one of the most astonishing art works in Patrizio's loft is of Hellenic provenance. The candle sculpture on the glass table next to the pool is by the Greek artist Liane Vassalou. The pillars are decorated with works by Lucio Fontana, the neon letters TAGE were designed by Maurizio Pellegrin, and the extensive collection of beautiful glass vases and bowls displayed on all kinds of surfaces throughout the building dates from the years between 1910 and 1960.

In line with Patrizio's rigorous minimalist principles, the kitchen is in black and white. The work surfaces are in *nero assoluto* stone and the tabletop rests on the base of a 1930s cooker. Similarly, the simplicity of his bedroom is reminiscent of a monk's cell – an attractive cell, it has to be said, and one with its own en-suite bathroom, complete with a barber's chair dating from 1910.

Apart from the unique swimming pool in the living room, this unusual house has two further surprises to offer: a charmingly romantic courtyard that nudges the venerable Botanical Garden, and an unexpectedly youthful motorbike, which leans casually against the wall in the hallway. 'I ride my Peugeot Geo into town like a horse, day after day. How would I get anywhere without it in this city?

ABOVE & OPPOSITE Patrizio Romano Paris loves to mix the traditional with the minimalist and modern. A Classical Roman torso adorns the corridor leading to the light-filled living area. The two conceptual paintings are by Laura Grisi.

LEFT & BELOW Patrizio loves bold colours and clean lines. The neon sculpture TAGE is designed by Maurizio Pellegrin, whereas the collection of glass vases and bowls by FontanArte, throughout the building, dates from between 1910 and 1960.

PREVIOUS PAGE & LEFT Patrizio Romano Paris is also a romantic – the courtyard bordering on the Botanical Garden is in charming contrast to his pared-down interiors.

BELOW LEFT One of the most astonishing art works in Patrizio's loft is the candle sculpture (on the glass table) by Greek artist Liane Vassalou. He used 10 tonnes of iron to replace the the dilapidated roof with a modern construction supported by iron girders.

OPPOSITE Striped mosaic-clad columns separate the dining room from the living area. Patrizio's chill-out zone, a black-and-white-tiled oasis, is dominated by a heated swimming pool complete with massage jets.

LEFT The bedroom has an en-suite bathroom, which is home to a barber's chair dating from 1910. Throughout the building, Patrizio had a mahogany floor laid directly onto the pressed earth. He likes to work with wood, which he appreciates for both its practicality and its beauty.

OPPOSITE The simplicity of Paris's bedroom is reminiscent of a monk's cell, which is in line with his rigorous minimalist design principles. His collections of old measuring instruments, toys and vessels are displayed on shelves above the beds, which are clothed in bedlinen from Souleiado.

1:6 URBAN RETRO

You know photographer Tim Brightmore's place is not going to be ordinary long before you reach it. Just behind London's King's Cross Station, in an area not always known for its stylish homes, a functional 1930s block stands next to a run-down car wash. A hi-tech control panel greets you at street level, then a utilitarian concrete and steel staircase. You wonder where it leads to.

He first viewed the place four years ago when the development first came onto the market, but felt it was too expensive. The deal went through a year later, when the agent offered Tim one of the last two units. Architects Ferhan Azman and Joyce Owens, known for creating simple, functional spaces, proved to be the perfect choice to realise Tim's vision of a combined living/work space. According to Owens, unlike many so-called lofts, Tim's place is the real thing: either people don't know what to do with the space and divide it up again, or a developer calls a space a loft when really it's an apartment.

Azman Owens was recommended to Tim by a friend. His brief was simple: as an advertising photographer, he needed as much space as possible for shooting, as well as places to put away his equipment, so creating an easy transition from working environment to relaxing living space. But he also wanted the essentials – a great kitchen, an energising bathroom, a tranquil bedroom, plus somewhere to eat.

Joyce says they found it a great challenge. 'We found fewer constraints and we were concentrating more on sustaining the quality of the light.' In order to keep the main space, which has windows on two sides, free for shooting, they decided that the living essentials had to run along the 50ft long opposite solid wall. Tim needed an office area, a darkroom for loading film, a tall cupboard for stashing rolled-up backgrounds, and another for storing photographic flats. Incredibly, all this (plus a laundry room) is located in a single run of cupboards. They have a variety of different handles, but all are painted the same pale grey, fading away to almost nothing. Come here early in the morning, before Tim has started work, and you see a smooth plane of floor-to-ceiling cupboard doors, but revisit at lunchtime, when Tim is shooting, and various doors will be open, each one revealing a super-functional cupboard. Slide one of the tall doors aside, and Tim's 'office' is revealed. Compact yet cosy, overhead shelves provide space for the stereo and files, there's a slab of built-in work surface, and room for his filing cabinet.

The bathroom was the only room which needed solid walls all around. It contains a neutral, no-nonsense walk-in shower with pale blue-grey mosaic tiles, a fixed glass shower screen and modern wall-mounted sink. The floor is one of Tim's special finds. If you look closely, you will see that it sparkles. 'It's a special nonslip floor that is often used in sports clubs,' he explains. Azman Owens suggested the rest of the bathroom fittings, but Tim had already spotted the basin he wanted in C.P. Hart.

The bedroom has one wall devoted to more cupboards, and what seems to be an intense, aqua-painted wall. In reality, the colour comes from paper roller blinds concealing a continuation of the studio's steel-framed glass wall. Although the blinds look as though they come from a specialist supplier, Tim made them himself from photographer's background paper. There is very little furniture – just a bed, bedside tables, and a 1970s swivel chair bought for £10 from a junk shop. Opposite the bed, and dividing the room from the main studio space, is an ingenious screen – a steel frame made to Azman Owens' spec, onto which Tim has stretched canvas. It is particularly clever because it works by dividing rather than blocking off, doubling up as a photographic background on the studio side.

Back in the main space, your eye is taken straight to the modern, functional lines of the kitchen. In a subtle shift of style, the doors here are painted the same pale grey of the bigger cupboards, but are handle-free. It's a kitchen of its time, yet not overly trendy. The Smeg oven and specially made hob are stainless steel, but the modernity is countered by a maple worktop and flooring. Clearly Azman Owens leave few stones unturned in their pursuit of perfection, for even the kitchen lights, nothing special in themselves, have been encased in galvanised metal to make them flush with the wall. 'We neverdo anything simply!' Joyce laughs.

What's also special about this kitchen is that it's marked out from the studio area by means of a low chunk of grey concrete wall. 'The builders used a timber mould for the concrete slab and it took on the grain of the wood,' Tim explains. Polished concrete on the floor runs through into the bedroom, with underfloor heating to keep it cosy in winter.

Surrounded by such expanses of glass and concrete, doesn't Tim ever feel overcome by too much light, or gloominess outside when the rain pours down? 'It's north-facing here so I get a constant, very gentle light,' he says and, if it's grey outside, the lighting has been specifically planned to create a pleasant ambience. What's more, the dining area always glows warmly with a wall of rich terracotta (Tim's chosen colour), whatever the weather. Set against the wall is an anodised Louis Poulsen pendant lamp, made in Germany.

Tim may have moved into a slickly designed shell, but he has well and truly stamped it with his own quirky, retro-chic look. Practically and aesthetically, Tim's requirements have been met to perfection.

ABOVE & OPPOSITE   Because the bathroom has no windows, the circular mirror above the wall-mounted basin was designed to be lit from behind. The loft is north-facing, so gets a constant gentle light, but the lighting in the loft, when required, creates a pleasant ambience. Dividing the bedroom from the main studio space is an ingenious screen, a steel frame over which Tim has stretched canvas and which doubles up as a photographic background on the studio side.

ABOVE The beautifully effective aqua blinds may look as though they come from a specialist shop but, in fact Tim made them himself from photographer's background paper.

ABOVE In the dining area, a terracotta-painted wall counterbalances the expanse of steel and glass, and adds warmth whatever the weather outside.

LEFT & ABOVE   The modern, functional lines of the kitchen are firmly stamped with Azman Owens'

characteristic look. It is marked out from the studio area by a low clunk of grey concrete wall, so

marvellously grained that it barely resembles concrete at all. The doors here are painted in the same grey

as the bigger cupboards in the loft, but this time are handle-free. The modernity of the Smeg oven and

stainless-steel hob is countered by a maple worktop. The smooth plane of floor-to-ceiling doors conceals

an array of super-functional cupboards, which house the owner's living and work essentials. There is not

a solid partition in sight.

1:7 PURE PERFECTION

An atmosphere of tranquillity and peace strikes you the moment you enter furniture designer Henri Becq's shop in Paris. This unusual experience emanates just as much from the designer himself as it does the furniture or the way it is presented. Slight and neat, with impeccable manners, Henri exudes a discreet air of serenity and calm. This acts as a magnet for the decorators and private clients who call on him with unfailing regularity. Today Henri is considered one of France's most exciting designers. He has two shops: one in the rue Jacob and another in the nearby rue de Seine.

He studied to be an *architecte d'intérieur* at the Ecole d'Art Moderne in Paris. 'You learn about perspective, how to do drawings and make plans – it has proved invaluable in my chosen career.' At the time Henri wanted to be an interior decorator, a career he pursued until he suddenly realised that his future lay in the closely associated world of furniture design. 'I have always loved modern furniture and I felt there was a gap in the market for an affordable range,' he recalls. To this end he set up shop in Paris and found an apartment in the old quarter of Paris.

Ten years later he moved the business to St Germain-des-Près: 'I loved living in the village atmosphere of the Marais but it was totally impractical to live at one end of Paris with a business at the other.' He swiftly secured business premises on the Left Bank, but finding suitable living accommodation proved to be more tricky. One day he came across a small area between the grand avenues and promenades of St Germain that had the villagey attributes he was looking for: narrow streets, wonderful shops and, most importantly, friendly residents. After nearly two years of searching, he eventually found himself a small apartment on the first floor of a seventeenth-century building in the heart of his chosen area. 'I thought it might be too noisy but I was captivated by the high ceilings and three floor-to-ceiling windows.'

Unperturbed by the beige, orange and brown colour scheme, Henri decided to play up the simplicity of the architecture, which had been updated in the 1960s. The fact there was no fireplace was not a problem, and the wall between the sitting and dining rooms had been taken down, creating one large space. 'The bathroom and the kitchen were minute, but the bedroom, located at the rear of the building overlooking a courtyard, was exceptionally quiet.'

Today the apartment is a tribute to Henry's beliefs: purity and simplicity plus a healthy respect for architecture. All he had to do was replace the floorboards with parquet tinted the same colour as the furniture, and paint the walls and woodwork white, which gave him a suitable background for displaying his furniture against. When it came to planning the space Henri had very definite ideas. 'Like all small apartments, it was important to maximise space and create a sense of continuity.'

OPPOSITE & ABOVE Three highly versatile rosewood book-cases line the end wall of the dining room. The square dining table in the centre of the room is surrounded by a set of linen-covered *Directoire-style* chairs.

Consequently, the double *salon* at the front of the apartment was turned into a practical open-plan sitting/dining room.

Henri always intended to furnish the apartment with his own designs, and accessorise the rooms with objects from the shop or commissions, set against a palette of black, brown, ecru and white. 'My own flat is an ideal place to try out prototypes,' he explains.

One of the sitting room's walls is dominated by an unusual triptych by a personal friend, Ariane Lassaigne. 'It was the first piece I commissioned and has proved an enormous success,' he states with pride. He then laid a dark-brown goatskin rug over most of the floor space, which instantly gave the room a warm luxurious feeling. Since the room was lacking a focal point, Henri grouped the furniture round the edge of the rug. 'To play up the effect I chose a day bed rather than a sofa. It's less bulky and doesn't monopolise the space.'

Although the apartment is neither cold nor minimalist, possessions are pared down and chosen uniquely for their shape. Each piece speaks for itself and plays a particular role – nothing is left to chance. In the sitting room, two clay pots and large matching plate by Kose are grouped to form an eye-catching display set against the simple background. 'I'm not acquisitive by nature ... I'm also extremely tidy, which is a real bonus in such a tiny space.'

White seat covers and curtains bordered with ecru taffeta highlight the overall theme in the dining room. To retain a sense of balance Henri designed a set of three tall and narrow bookcases, placed in a row along the end wall. It is a more versatile arrangement as they can be used in a variety of ways. A square dining table surrounded by a set of newly designed chairs stands in the centre of the room, and proves to be an ideal place for Henri to browse over his new designs.

A small internal lobby leads to the bedroom, which is dominated by the bed with its chic sycamore bedhead. Crisp white bedlinen perfectly complements the rich-brown cashmere throw. A pair of lamps from the Modenature collection sit atop the two bedside tables.

Mirrors and black-and-white photographs embellish the white-tiled walls of the adjacent bathroom. 'There wasn't a great deal you could do in such a small room except make it functional and practical,' maintains Henri. 'As I rarely take a shower I was able to hang pictures on the wall above the bath.'

Totally at ease with himself and his surroundings, Henri says he would be perfectly happy to stay in the apartment for the rest of his days. 'I could be tempted by a large lofty space, I suppose,' he admits. 'But until that comes along I'm perfectly happy to stay put.'

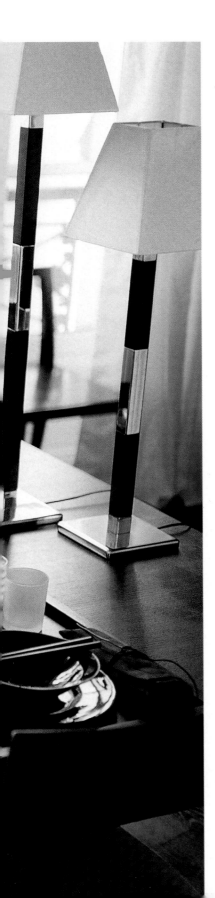

LEFT & ABOVE For Henri Becq, 'a square table is the modern version of the round table', and here it proves an ideal space for him to browse his new designs. The majority of the tableware displayed here was designed exclusively for the Modenature collection. The brown linen table napkins are by Murielle Grateau.

ABOVE & RIGHT One wall of the sitting room is largely dominated by an unusual triptych by Ariane Lassaigne, the first piece Henri ever commissioned. The television is housed by a Chinese-style cabinet, on which stands a vase designed by Kaki Kroeber for Modenature. A suede day bed was chosen instead of a sofa, as it is less bulky and doesn't monopolise the space. In the foreground is a pair of 1930s chairs designed by de Rielvelt.

OPPOSITE & ABOVE In the sitting room, two clay pots and a large matching plate by Kose are perfectly grouped to form an eye-catching display set against the simple white background. A suede-covered chair sits comfily next to them. The dark-brown goatskin rug, chosen to complement the colours of the furniture and upholstery, takes up most of the room's floor space. Henri grouped the furniture around the edge of the rug to give the room a focal point.

LEFT & ABOVE The bed, with its chic sycamore bedhead, dominates the bedroom. On either side, two small tables are topped with a pair of lamps from the Modenature collection, while the white bedlinen complements the brown cashmere perfectly. The white-tiled walls in the bathroom are embellished with mirrors and black-and-white photographs. Henri was even able to hang pictures on the wall above the bath, since the shower is rarely used.

2:0 THE GENTLEMAN

Of all the male style tribes, that of the gentleman is perhaps the oldest and most instantly recognisable. There are certain features that we associate almost exclusively with the gentleman and his abode, and there are particular words we use to describe his lifestyle: leisured, traditional, timeless, refined. Many writers and cultural authorities have attempted to define the gentleman and his style. 'He cannot be a gentleman which loveth not a dog,' stated John Northbrooke rather simplistically in 1577. A more expansive definition can be found a century later, in 1668, in the words of Thomas Shadwell: 'The qualifications of a fine gentleman are to eat *à la mode*, drink champagne, dance jigs and play at tennis.' The same sentiment was echoed by Oscar Wilde two hundred years on in *The Importance of Being Earnest*: 'One's duty as a gentleman should never interfere with one's pleasure in the slightest degree.'

The *Oxford English Dictionary* lists several meanings for the term 'gentleman', of which this comes first: 'A man of gentle birth, or having the same heraldic status as those of gentle birth; properly, one who is entitled to bear arms, though not ranking among the nobility, but also applied to a person of distinction without precise definition of rank.' This chiefly historical definition is followed by one which rings more familiar in modern times: 'A man of superior position in society, or having the habits of life indicative of this; often, one whose means enable him to live in easy circumstances without engaging in trade, a man of money and leisure.' Indeed, the gentleman's money and leisure make him perfectly suited to bachelordom. He has both the means and the time to pursue the unencumbered life of the single man. Although the gentleman may not always remain a bachelor, he will certainly play out the role with enthusiasm while single. If he does marry, he is sure to keep some aspects of his bachelor life, retaining private space and private time within the domestic sphere.

The gentleman's pursuit of leisure is carried out almost exclusively in the countryside. Historically, the English gentleman's abode was his estate in the countryside. A town house in London was a necessity for political reasons – to retain ties with the influential men who governed the fate of landowners – but the country was always the preferred place of residence. It is this love for all things country that remains the most telling characteristic of the gentleman and his style. It is seen most clearly in his choice of dress. The English gentleman was for nearly two hundred years the leading arbiter of taste in the Western world, with a wardrobe based around the traditional country sports. Fabrics were utilitarian and tailoring was devised with function foremost in mind.

Once perfected, these styles changed little. The eighteenth-century riding coat, for example, was high-collared, fitted to the waist with a full skirt. It was designed to be worn in all weather conditions and facilitate horse riding. It quickly became a classic, and is still the model for today's formal frock coat. The gentleman's sense of style is consistent and regulated. There is no room for the expressiveness or flamboyance sported by other men, either in their dress or their homes. Family lineage, education at the best schools, travels abroad and links with the upper echelons of society underpin the gentleman's personal style. A keen sense of tradition informs and shapes his carefully constructed world.

For the uninitiated, Debrett's guide to manners and etiquette provides an insight into the world of gentlemanly style. On the wearing of suits, for example, DeBrett's advises: 'Town suits should be of good quality cloth – ideally all-wool worsted – and sub-dued in colour. If patterned, the design should be discreet – pinstripes, birdseyes, pinheads or unfussy checks are best – and although Oxford grey and navy are the most traditional suit colours, brown is also popular. Tweed suits, though acceptable, are not often seen in cities, except possibly on Fridays when the wearer is going to the country for the weekend. A combination of sports jacket and flannel trousers in town usually means the wearer is European or American.' Classic and timeless, these are the watchwords of both the gentleman's wardrobe and his home.

The qualities which govern the gentleman's dress can also be found in his choice of interior. He will choose solid, comfortable furnishings made by hand from English hardwoods such as oak, chestnut and beech. He will lend every room a sense of tradition in the form of family portraits or treasured antique pieces. More often than not he will decorate with discreet patterns and plain colours. Essential to any gentleman's abode is the book-lined study – testament to the owner's excellent education and appreciation of history.

Touches of the countryside will often be present, even in a town house or apartment. The best-quality wool carpets or rugs will line the halls and rooms, in colours meant to reflect nature yet also to withstand a gentleman's muddy riding boots – forest green or deep, autumnal red. A traditional floral wallcovering may bring the delights of pastoral England indoors, as may the painting of a racehorse or favourite landscape. The influence of the countryside may also be present in the cosy warmth of a sitting room with well-stuffed couch, ample cushions, rugs, heavy drapes and a fireplace.

Overall, the gentleman's home is designed to create a harmonious and refined environment. There are no eye-catching design features nor modernist sensibilities; no attention-grabbing light fittings or jarring colours. All elements are carefully chosen to reflect the owner's good taste and, above all, his respect for tradition.

2:1 TIMELESS OPULENCE

Alidad Mahloudji and his family left Iran in the 1960s and, apart from a short spell in Switzerland, he has lived in London ever since. Based in a Mayfair apartment, he has a flourishing interior decorating practice, working alongside a small, dedicated team. His career took off when he took an art course at Sotheby's, then worked there for several more years. One day he locked himself in the room with all auction pieces and spent hours transforming the place into something magical. The sale that followed was a resounding success, so he continued to play decorator for his department, and found himself increasingly interested in the display rather than the objects themselves.

His passion for antiques had led him into the world of interior decoration, and before he knew it he was dealing with clients in the UK and abroad. He already loved rich, warm colours and living in England taught him how to appreciate comfort. By looking and observing wherever he went, he was able to learn about architecture and architectural detailing, and today he travels all over the world, redesigning and creating some of the most desirable homes imaginable. 'Having had an international upbringing myself, I am able to draw on different styles and tastes – from the East to the West.' To start with, he gets to know his clients and the way they like to live. 'I'm always looking ahead. I want the decoration to last for decades rather than years. It has to be something you can enjoy and build on.'

In his own home Alidad has created a timeless effect, which has matured and evolved over the last twenty years. When he first saw the property, he was determined to have it, despite only having three rooms. Five years later, he bought the apartment next door, which gave him the opportunity to create a larger, more flexible layout. He was still working at Sotheby's at the time, and hadn't even thought about becoming a decorator.

He knew that he had to incorporate a red room somewhere, and today large double doors connect the drawing room and library – the longed-for red room and heart of the house. This is Alidad at its best – comfortable and sublimely luxurious. Deep-red hand-painted walls, based on designs seen in mosques and other buildings in the Middle East, have aged to perfection. Different shades of red have been used in the room and, though they blend, clash and jar, somehow they all work wonderfully together. Bookcases painted the colour of the walls flank the window and the fireplace, exuding a comfortable effect that harmonises with the colours and textures in the room. Alidad likes to create different atmospheres for different times of the day and for different rooms, and he is very conscious of the five senses in his interior decoration. For him, it is also important to consider the style and period of the house.

In the morning the sun streams into the adjoining sitting room. 'You need [both] a dark and a light room in a house to make it really work, he explains ' A magnificent nineteenth-century Persian carpet covers the wooden floorboards, which have been painted around the edges to accentuate the carpet pattern. The room was large enough to accommodate two seating areas, with a sofa placed against the wall opposite the fireplace and banquette seating under the window. This gave him the freedom to use the remaining space as he wished. A magnificent eighteenth-century velvet Mogul fabric hangs above the sofa (Alidad often uses textiles rather than paintings – they cost far less and are equally aesthetically pleasing).

Alidad firmly believes that unless you have a room to spare the dining room is dead space, but if you have room, 'Don't be afraid to create something completely mad – it's the only room in the house where you can.' His own dining room is a triumph, with a trompe l'oeil ceiling and stamped and gilded leather walls in shades of red, gold and green, a move that allowed him to create a highly dramatic effect. 'Leather walls were very popular in the seventeenth and eighteenth centuries and have a wonderful texture, which you can embellish with large patterns and masses of silver and gold.' As the room is fairly small, Alidad put an enormous freestanding bookcase at one end, creating an illusion of height and overall balance. 'One overscaled piece ... pushes the walls back and makes the room appear much larger,' he says, adding that ' ... you can create an amazing illusion for very little. Combine inexpensive things with a few good pieces, and mix old and new. If everything is too perfect, it looks dull – you are not trying to create a museum but a home!'

Alidad installed a handsome late nineteenth-century fireplace in the bedroom, and painted the walls a glorious shade of bottle green, then varnished them to create a shiny effect. He incorporated lots of old fabrics in bold red and green shades (a delicious combination), adding a wonderful blue and red Zeigler carpet. To one side of the fireplace a slipper chair is upholstered in red-and-beige-striped needlework, while another is covered in old leather with a throw casually draped over it. The bed has a magnificent eighteenth-century red velvet bedcover complete with original gold braid. Against one wall, an old sofa upholstered in a magnificent green self-patterned Fortuny fabric was an impulsive buy.

At the end of the day it's his red room that Alidad pines for whenever he leaves home. It is the first place he goes to; where he thinks and listens to music, or just sit for the sheer pleasure of being there.' It also encompasses everything he likes best in decoration, its style is pure Alidad – opulent with jewel-like colours, exquisite textiles and well-loved antiques.

ABOVE & OPPOSITE Dining chez Alidad is an unforgettable experience – amidst the glitter and glitz of several hundred candles and masses of silver and gold, guests can luxuriate in the opulent surroundings. It is all about creating a night of fantasy where people can relax and enjoy themselves.

OPPOSITE   Alidad is highly conscous of the five senses. When you walk into a room – even the hallway – you are aware not only of its visual appeal, but gentle music plays in the background, there are glorious fabrics to feel and stroke, and exotic aromas emanate from flowers and candles.

RIGHT   Alidad's sense of daring and style is evident throughout the library. His first move was to take out the existing fireplace and replace it with a large white marble example.

ABOVE & RIGHT Accentuate the fact that a room is really dark by
using strong, bold colours. Alidad's library contains sofas, cushions
and chairs covered in kilims and needlepoint, both old and new, and
mixes pattern upon pattern, texture upon texture.

OPPOSITE & ABOVE The sitting room is light and bright, with two large windows and a door leading onto a tiny balcony. Alidad

has exacerbated this feeling of brightness by introducing a warm yellow ochre to the walls and woodwork painted the colour of stone.

Old texttiles that have faded over the years are now used as tablecloths, and cushions have taken on a personality and charm of their

own. The room is large enough to accommodate two distinct seating areas.

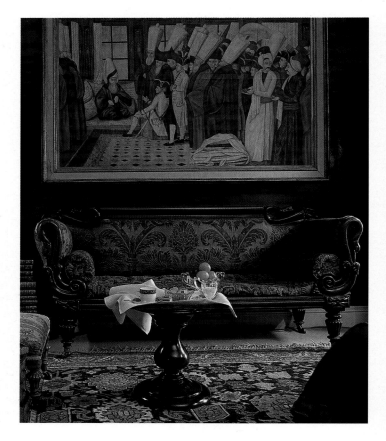

ABOVE & RIGHT   A handsome late nineteenth-century fireplace has been installed in the bedroom. The walls were painted a glorious shade of bottle green, then varnished to create a shiny effect. The room needed many different textures to bring it to life – lots of fabrics in bold greens and reds appear on both the walls and the furniture.

2:2 CONTEMPORARY CLASSICAL

Even as a child Jean-Pierre Calvagrac had a passion for antiques and decoration. He studied Law, and had never dreamed of becoming an interior decorator. He started his career working for antiques dealers and decorators during the school holidays, and in 1984 he moved to Paris, where he worked for Ralph Lauren's Home Collection – an inspired move that kick-started his chosen career.

Today he has a home in Paris and also runs a successful interior decorating business based there. 'I have an excellent team and working with them has helped me to learn about all the different aspects of the business; as a result my ideas and visual appreciation have matured and improved,' explains Jean-Pierre. 'It's not easy for people with different ideas to work together but we all complement each other perfectly.'

A few years ago he purchased a large apartment in the old part of the city – a spacious fifth-floor apartment on one corner of a nineteenth-century Hausmann building overlooking the place de la Bastille. When he first saw the flat, Jean-Pierre was suitably impressed with the layout and the scale of the rooms. Although the apartment needed modernising, the basic structure hadn't really changed. The rooms were quite small and the ceilings relatively low, but he saw endless possibilities.

It wasn't until he moved in that Jean-Pierre became fully aware of the magnificent *enfilade* of rooms running down one entire side of the building – heavy oak furniture had up till then concealed the open-plan nature of the property. He decided to open up the space and allow one room to flow into the next without interruption. Fortunately, the original fireplaces were still in place, although the floors needed sanding and polishing to bring them to life. Throughout the apartment windows were repaired and cornices and mouldings replaced. Services were updated, the kitchen relocated and a second bathroom installed. 'I decided to make use of the corridors and doorways to emphasise the various perspectives,' he explains. 'Now you can see into more than one room at the same time, which gives the apartment a wonderfully airy feel.'

When Jean-Pierre first took over the flat the rooms were painted in true 1960s colours: lime green, fuchsia and cobalt blue: 'I thought 'How awful' and immediately painted everything white,' he recalls. But without colour the rooms lacked personality. 'I painted the sitting room a glorious shade of blue but it made the other rooms look cold and out of place,' explains Jean-Pierre. He needed good, strong colours that would coexist harmoniously but, not surprisingly, the *enfilade* presented a problem, since so many rooms were visible at the same time. Each room needed to stand out, yet also blend in, and it took months of trying one colour after another before a satisfactory conclusion was reached.

Now, the moment you enter the flat you know you that have chanced upon something unique. 'The idea was to have an interior that wouldn't date, so mixing the old with the new and using different periods seemed the obvious thing to do,' he explains. But it was also important to retain a link between the decoration and the occupants; otherwise a room can look impersonal. Most important, it needs a sense of humour.

Large double doors lead from the aubergine hall into the oval drawing room, where three sets of French doors provide access to a balcony overlooking the place de la Bastille. In contrast to the rest of the apartment this room has a cool, minimal appeal with white walls and simple wooden floors. The room may be traditional but it has a quirky edge. 'It's incredibly versatile,' explains Jean-Pierre. 'Wonderful for entertaining on a grand or intimate scale.'

From here, looking down the *enfilade* towards a small sitting room at the far end, the eye travels through an unusually striking combination of periods and designs, each decoratively displayed against a background of bold colour. The first room is the smallest in the apartment and was the last to be decorated. Because most of the rooms in the flat are open-plan, Jean-Pierre had difficulty choosing appropriate colours for the walls. He settled eventually on a wonderful shade of terracotta, which seemed to unify all the colours.

The next room is the bedroom. 'My intention here was to combine dark-grey walls with dark-brown taffeta curtains from my previous home,' explains Jean-Pierre. 'Sadly, every grey I tried developed a greenish tinge so in desperation we painted the walls black.' The result was a triumph: 'It provided exactly the atmosphere I had in mind and made the room very cosy and romantic.' However, a pair of 1940s-style screens flanking a bust of William I of Holland behind the bed was specially made and positioned to break up the symmetry of the room.'

At the end of the *enfilade* is the purple sitting room, which is used for relaxing, listening to music or watching the television. The room has an unexpected Oriental ambience, but 'for some unexplained reason anything painted gold looked dated and out of place', he explains. To overcome the problem he painted most of the pieces white, and 'Now the garden urn looks as if it has come straight out of a castle in Sweden.' Some of the pieces he bought on a whim, while others were meticulously planned.

Whatever the weather or the time of the year, Jean-Pierre can be sure of a cheerful welcome every time he enters the apartment. 'It's such a pleasure to wander from room to room soaking up the atmosphere and enjoying the colours.'

ABOVE & OPPOSITE   Jean-Pierre Calvagrac's spacious Parisian apartment is on one corner of a nineteenth-century Hausmann building overlooking the place de la Bastille, in the old part of the city. When he first saw the flat, he was impressed by its layout and scale, and now, 'The moment you walk through the front door, you feel cocooned in a blanket of comfort and warmth,' he maintains.

OPPOSITE & ABOVE An eye-catching blend of versatility and colour creates a home that is up-to-the

minute yet elegant, but with a Classical slant. Almost all of the furnishings in Jean-Pierre's bedroom –

including a portrait of Louis XVI, a Louis XVI secretaire and a handsome chandelier – came from the room

he occupied as a boy.

RIGHT   To create an impression of grandeur and space, an entire wall in the small sitting room was covered with square mirror tiles. A section of floor-to-dado-rail panelling has been painted white to emphasise the colour of the walls. The furnishings are mainly from the 1940s, their colours and shapes chosen especially for the room.

PREVIOUS PAGE, OPPOSITE & ABOVE   The purple sitting room, situated at the end of the line

of rooms, is used for reading, listening to music or watching television. It has an unexpected Oriental

ambience verging on 1970s psychedelia, and is anchored by splashes of white. By adding contempo-

rary Chinese accessories such as a turquoise silk lantern or red-lacquered tables – chosen for their shape,

not their pedigree – the room has acquired a sense of balance and proportion.

LEFT & ABOVE By combining unusual colours with the old and the new in a modern yet traditional setting, the apartment takes on a relaxed and contemporary ambience. In the hall, for example, deep aubergine walls are complemented by sharp white woodwork. To emphasise the effect, a row of glass plinths supporting antique busts has been placed along one wall, which creates the feel of a gallery.

OPPOSITE & ABOVE   The reception room is the heart of Jean-Pierre's apartment, and is used

as a sitting room, dining room, hall, or as somewhere to plonk belongings. The decoration is based

around the colours of a beautiful *Directoire* trumeau found in the attic of his parents' house. He paint-

ed the walls a glorious shade of Wedgwood blue, a colour taken from the painting on the mirror.

ABOVE & OPPOSITE Doric columns, from Jean-Pierré's previous home, give the reception room an air of importance, while in the centre of the room a charming Louis-Philippe table, surrounded by a set of Empire chairs, is offset by a handsome chaise-longue upholstered in raspberry-red silk.

LEFT & ABOVE The oval drawing room is the most traditional room in the flat, but still retains a distinctly quirky edge. Materials such as glass, mirror and metal combine with shiny fabrics like satin and silk organza to highlight the room's sophisticated simplicity.

LEFT & ABOVE Three sets of French doors in the oval drawing room provide access to a small balcony overlooking the place de la Bastille. In contrast to the rest of the apartment, this room has a cool, almost minimal appeal, with white walls and simple wooden floors.

2:3 DARKNESS & LIGHT

After studying Law, Swiss-born interior decorator Christophe Gollut's career took a complete U-turn – he moved to London to take a course at the Inchbald School of Design. 'Coming from an artistic background, I found design was more to my taste,' he recalls. 'I simply adored it.' Once he received his diploma, Christophe bought a share in a decorating business in London's Fulham Road, and when his partners wanted to disband the company, in 1971, Christophe's father stepped in and bought the business for him. 'In effect, I have worked from the same premises since 1969, which must be some sort of a record,' he claims. Christophe's work takes him all over the world and his style remains virtually unchanged: eclectic, a tad eccentric, yet incredibly cosy and warm, with a wonderful sense of balance and style. 'I like using lots of different textiles combined with richly coloured or subtly faded fabrics and good antiques,' he explains.

When the lease on his previous flat came to an end, he decided to look for something relatively similar – somewhere on the first floor, with a balcony, a large reception room and one or two bedrooms. He found what he wanted a few days later and snapped it up. The flat had been done up in the 1960s and the decoration was appalling, but Christophe could see its potential. The rabbit warren of tiny rooms was transformed into a magnificent apartment. Once the partition walls were taken down and a redundant lift shaft in the drawing room was removed, the original proportions were revealed. So, too, was a magnificent floor-to-ceiling window, and a three-windowed bay giving onto a large, wide balcony.

Christophe knew exactly what he wanted. 'I'm an instant decorator but I like things that last ... I can visualise a room exactly as it will be when finished in a split second. For example, the decoration here hasn't changed for twelve years and I like it just as much – maybe even more.' By making a double doors from the drawing room into an adjacent bedroom, he was able to create a second reception room, to be used as a dining room/kitchen or study. Initially, a small door next to the main drawing-room entrance revealed a long, narrow corridor that gave access to the bedrooms and bathroom at the rear of the flat. By blocking it off in the drawing room and making another entrance halfway down, Christophe gained enough space to build a large cupboard and install a minute (6ft by 2$^{1/2}$ft) kitchen in a recess in the new dining room. This kitchen boasts a fridge, plus oven with worktop and hotplates. A second cupboard houses the sink, cutlery and china.

Almost everything in the drawing room needed repairing or replacing. Christophe installed a magnificent late eighteenth-century French marble fireplace, replaced the broken and damaged moulding, and sanded and limed the original wood floor. 'I painted the walls a wonderful shade of green to complement the array of different pinks found in the fabrics, cushions and rugs.' Now, although the room is awash with colour, nothing seems to jar or dominate. A carefully selected combination of objects emphasises Christophe's exquisite taste. The ivory silk taffeta curtains are rarely drawn, as the flat is not overlooked and the glare of the sun is diffused by off-white roller blinds. 'It's wonderful in the summer, as you can throw open the French windows and wander out onto the balcony, yet in winter it's incredibly cosy, with a fire and all those lovely warm colours to cheer you up,' he explains.

Large double doors lead into the dining-room-cum-study. Here the walls are covered in a bold-striped damask in shades of green, red and honey; below the dado rail green chenille velvet lines the walls. 'All the woodwork was marbleised and the doors given a *faux bois* treatment by artist Ernesto Signorelli,' explains Christophe. This is a dark room, and the perfect antidote to the bright light of the drawing room. His motto is, 'If it's dark, make it darker'. Hence walls lined with groups of mid- to late nineteenth-century Swiss paintings and a looking glass acquired by Christophe's grandparents. Flanking one of the banquettes is a magnificent pair of eighteenth-century Italian marble-topped console tables from Grant White that add a pleasing touch of glamour.

The room relies heavily on light from the drawing room, so rather than curtains Christophe decorated the small rectangular window with a length of antique lace embellished with a crest and a lion, topped by a gorgeously decorative gilt pelmet. This is where he conceals his tiny kitchen, behind double doors in a space that was once part of the corridor.

A decorative nineteenth-century curtain made into a *portière* forms the entrance to the passage that leads to the master bedroom and bathroom, at the rear of the apartment. 'The first time I saw the bedroom I decided it was going to be blue and white,' he recalls. The ceiling has been painted to resemble the sky, with puffy white clouds and fake blinds that give it a tented effect. He decided to treat himself by placing the bed in the bay window, which overlooks one of the most beautiful gardens in London.

Along the corridor is the bathroom, with its stained-glass windows. Although he is not a stained-glass fan, Christophe decided to keep it and decorate the room around it – hence green-painted walls, a green *faux*-marble bath surround and piles of fluffy green towels.

The moment you enter Christophe's front door you feel at ease. This may, of course, have something to so with the fact that he is one of those rare individuals who oozes genuine charm and is equally at home with himself as he is with others. But one must also pay tribute to the decoration: a lifetime's work that is lived in and loved to the full.

ABOVE & OPPPOSITE Although the drawing room is awash with different colours – some rich, some bold – nothing seems to jar or dominate. The ivory silk taffeta curtains are rarely drawn, seeing as the flat is not overlooked, and the glare of the sun is diffused by off-white roller blinds.

ABOVE & RIGHT A pair of magnificent floor-to-ceiling windows in the drawing room give onto a large balcony that spans the entire width of the flat. The whole room is bathed in light, which is lovely in summer – Christophe can simply throw open the windows and wander out onto the balcony.

LEFT Most of the furniture in the drawing room came from Christophe's previous flat, but the English bookcase and round table in the corner were new. To complement the array of pinks found in the fabrics, cushions and rugs, he painted the walls a wonderful shade of green.

ABOVE & OPPOSITE In the drawing room, a carefully selected combination of paintings and mirrors, furniture and objects emphasises Christophe's exquisite taste. Since there were no restrictions – almost everything in the room needed replacing or repairing – he installed a magnificent late eighteenth-century French marble fireplace.

OPPOSITE & RIGHT   The dining-room-cum-study is dark, representing a perfect antidote to the bright drawing room – seen through the large double doors –the walls are covered in a bold-striped damask in shades of red, green and honey and below the dado rail, green chenille velvet lines the walls. Christophe's motto is, 'If it's dark, make it darker' – hence the walls are lined with groups of nineteenth-century paintings and looking glasses acquired by his grandparents.

RIGHT A simple round table stands in the centre of the dining-room-cum-study, while banquettes and dining chairs are placed against the wall. Flanking one of the banquettes is a pair of eighteenth-century Italian marble-topped console tables that add a pleasing touch of glamour.

LEFT & OPPOSITE He put the bed in the bay window, so he can lie and gaze at the garden when he wakes up in the morning. Ivory silk curtains and Norfolk rush matting perfectly contribute to the bedroom's blue-and-white design scheme. Christophe admits that he occasionally has to water the matting, to make sure it does not dry out and crack up.

LEFT The master bedroom and bathroom is located near the rear of the apartment. Christophe wanted the room to be blue and white, so the ceiling was painted to resemble the sky, with white puffy clouds and fake blinds.

3:0 THE AESTHETE

The terms 'bachelor' and 'aesthete' are very well suited. Who better to appreciate 'art for art's sake' than the single male with money to spend on 'art' and with time to acquire its appreciation – so much more challenging for the married man surrounded by the household clutter and chaos that comes inevitably with children. He may be lucky enough to have a den or study to retreat to – a place where everything is just as he would like it. But these men are in the minority – the married man's domestic domain is essentially one of compromise.

The bachelor, on the other hand, is free to arrange his living space just as he would like it. This is the ideal scenario for the aesthete – to be able to materialise his ideas about art and taste in his personal style. The aesthete's style is the most uncompromising of all, requiring time and dedication to bring it to fruition. If the true definition is adhered to, the aesthete 'professes a special appreciation of what is beautiful, and endeavours to carry his ideas of beauty into practical manifestation.' The aesthete in his purest form is devoted to the study of aesthetics: the philosophy or theory of taste. To make that theory come alive, in what he wears or where he lives, even what he eats and drinks, is the aesthete's challenge. It is a challenge most of us would be eager to try, for it connotes a life of luxury, of devotion to quality and beauty at every level of living.

The Aesthetics movement itself dates back to the late eighteenth century, when the German philosophers Baumgarten and Kant developed a philosophical theory of the beautiful. These ideas would be revisited a century later, in the Aesthetics movement of the late nineteenth-century English artists and writers. They took as their credo 'art for art's sake.' In Sir W. Hamilton's 1882 study of the movement, he described the aesthetes as: 'they who pride themselves in having found out what is the really beautiful in nature and art, their faculties and tastes being educated up to the point necessary for the full appreciation of such qualities'.

But of all the historical subcultures associated with the idea of aesthetics, perhaps the most vivid is that of the Dandy. While not directly connected to the Aesthetic movement, the dandy embraced the notions of taste and beauty. In essence, dandyism was a movement devoted to personal style. The French philosopher Balzac mused on the meaning of the dandy in his famous 1830 manifesto Traité de le vie élégante,(or *Treatise of an Elegant Life*),in which he makes various declarations on living a stylish life. 'The man of taste must always know how to reduce his needs to the most simple'; 'Multiplicity of colours will be in bad taste.'; and even more strident: ' We ...owe to Brummell, the philosophical inductions by which we have demonstrated how much elegant life is tied to the perfection of all human society.'

The Brummell he refers to is, of course, George 'Beau' Brummell, the legendary English dandy of the late eighteenth and early nineteenth centuries. To him and his dandies, style was everything – extravagance was out and understatement was in; his sober but immaculate taste in clothing is still seen by many as the high point of English male fashion. Brummell's trick was to spend hours of painstaking attention to his dress and toilette, and then appear as though it was all artlessly created. Described as 'the most elegant man in the world' Brummell's champions ranged from the Prince of Wales, who reputedly sat at Brummell's feet as he dressed himself for the day, to Lord Byron, who described him as exuding 'that certain exquisite propriety.' One essayist of the time wrote that Brummell 'remained dressed in an irreproachable fashion; but he subdued the colours of his clothes, simplified their cut and wore them without thinking ... a dandy can spend ... ten hours at his toilette, but once it is done he forgets it. It is others who must perceive that he is well dressed.' Even Virginia Woolf counted herself an admirer: 'The grace of his carriage was so astounding ... Everybody looked overdressed or badly dressed – some indeed looked positively dirty – beside him. His clothes seemed to melt into each other with the perfection of their cut and the quiet harmony of their colour. Without a single point of emphasis everything was distinguished ... '

The standards set by Brummel have remained largely in place over the intervening years. Even now, the aesthetics of contemporary male fashion are not too far away from 'Beau's' cultured and refined appearance, despite today's informal standards. The modern aesthete more than likely dresses in sombre, muted shades – black or beige – and in beautifully cut and luxurious fabrics; nothing too flashy or glitzy. And the aesthetic ideals for furnishing the interior are likewise inspired by ideas of elegance and artistic beauty. The aesthete's home is meticulously planned and executed in the best possible taste, although it never appears contrived. Like the aesthete himself, the domestic sphere is beautifully and thoughtfully maintained. Refined, expensive and highly individualistic, it never fails to make an impression.

3:1 SUMPTUOUS SIMPLICITY

Paris-based interior architect Frédéric Mechiche inherited his love of architecture and decoration from his parents. 'My father ... was passionate about architecture.' He lived a lifestyle considered to be rather avant garde at the time: 'My mother hated anything remotely ostentatious and ... I grew up surrounded by things that were refined yet very simple, which made a lasting impression on me.' His free time as a child was spent visiting castles, stately homes, antique shops and flea markets.

When asked what he wanted to do when he left school, Frédéric replied, 'Why, decoration and architecture, of course,' so it is not a surprise that today he is France's most innovative decorator, with commissions from all over the world. He is able to recreate any style of architecture and decoration, from a simple cottage to a grand chateau, a house in the country to a loft or modern flat. Whatever the size or location of a project, Frédéric has one basic rule: first create the perfect base, *then* plan the decoration. Mood or atmosphere can be introduced in many ways, he says, but the base stays the same.

After spending more than a decade living in a magnificent loft in the old part of Paris, Frédéric decided it was time for a another challenge. But finding a suitable alternative was not easy. 'I am only happy living in the heart of a city,' he says. 'Not for me the busy boulevards with cars roaring up and down day and night. I prefer a village atmosphere with small shops and the sound of people laughing in the street.' When he was shown a rabbit warren of small apartments on the top two floors of a part fourteenth-century, part-1960s building, he decided to take the lot. Knowing he could transform them into what he was looking for, Frédéric proceeded to rip out everything, from the partition walls to the windows, the staircases and the doors, until all that remained were the exterior walls. He first set about planning the basic structure, aiming to use all, not just part of the space. Once the architectural base was in place, he injected his own brand of magic and within the limited confines of a nondescript shell, a magnificent *Directoire*-style town house began to emerge where (apart from one or two minor details) everything is authentic. Panelling rescued from an eighteenth-century country post office has been reconstructed with a surgeon's precision to fit the rooms. 'Errors of proportion are unforgivable,' he insists. 'The same applies to door frames and cornices.' Indeed, it is the elegant simplicity of the panelling and the appropriate architectural details that unify the scheme.

Today the apartment is a *tour de force*. When asked why, in a city brimming with late eighteenth-century apartments, he bothered gutting a pretty uninspiring building, only to replace it with something that could easily be found in another *quartier*, he says, 'Why not! I adore the location ... It gave me a unique opportunity to organise my space exactly as I wanted it.'

Throughout the apartment a series of rooms that are neither too large nor too high-ceilinged flow one into the other, flooded with light from a run of south-facing *Directoire* windows. Frédéric maintains that the strong, rather severe lines of the *Directoire* period look almost contemporary against the apartment's modern art and interiors. The sitting room is a total triumph – whitewashed panelling, floorboards covered with seagrass rugs, and straw blinds creating a soft overall light, all unify the scheme. 'Most of the furniture is from different countries and of varying periods,' he explains, adding that he likes to mix old and new, and high-quality items with funny little souvenirs, because it gives a room personality and charm.

Compared to the rest of the apartment, the bedroom is relatively minimal. 'I wanted a spacious room, with plenty of daylight,' says Frédéric, who chose a bold wide black-and-white-striped fabric for the bedhead and valance, which perfectly plays up the simple white background perfectly. An eighteenth-century oak parquet floor, which originally came from another room in the flat, was painstakingly moved into the bedroom piece by piece. The adjoining bathroom is dominated by a magnificent nineteenth-century zinc bath with painted *faux bois* decoration. Large mirrored doors contain the enormous shower room, where heated walls and towel rails ensure continual warmth. 'The bath is my fantasy,' says Frédéric. 'It's wonderful to have a long soak while listening to a good piece of music.'

Double doors connect the dining room with the kitchen, and a pair of doors leading from the dining room into the library allow guests to circulate with ease. 'For years I have dreamed of a dining-room which is a cross between a café and a picture gallery,' says Frédéric. 'I wanted to create a kind of 'picnic' atmosphere where guests can wear jeans or dinner jackets without feeling ill at ease.' The walls, painted a soft greyish mauve, are covered with a collection of photographs, drawings and 1940s watercolours. The elegant new staircase sweeps into the large, open library. It is the heart of the home, a neutral zone containing organised clutter dedicated to writing and reading. Built-in shelves under the stairs are crammed with a collection of books, while drawings, photographs and sketches are propped against walls and on shelves. One example of Frédéric's attention to detail is a mauve day bed by the window next to the dining room, linked to the far side of the room by a oil painting resting against the bookshelves.

'I love this apartment,' declares Frédéric with passion. 'It suits my lifestyle to perfection. I use and enjoy every inch of the space and derive enormous pleasure walking from one room into another – which is what I have to do, because of the way I planned it.'

ABOVE & OPPOSITE In the dining room, groups of nineteenth-century benches and seats upholstered in black-and-white stripes merge with wire-backed chairs and metal tables to create a street café effect. The walls – painted a soft greyish mauve – are covered with a collection of art works.

OPPOSITE & ABOVE Throughout the sitting room, Frédéric has planned a careful juxtaposition of contrasting styles – a sculpture by Dubuffet, drawings by Miró and masks from Zaire. He likes mixing old with new, and good-quality pieces with funny little souvenirs. Frédéric was keen to make sure the new staircase blended in properly, so he wore down the steps with a sanding machine, to create the impression of age.

ABOVE & OPPOSITE The key to the sitting room is versatility: it contains lots of chairs and small tables, which prove useful when it comes to entertaining. Leading off the sitting room is the gym, where Frédéric exercises surrounded by sumptuous works of art. He deliberately chose strong paintings and bold sculptures that would complement the heavy gym machines.

OPPOSITE & ABOVE Flanked by a pair of *Directoire* grisailles, a magnificent eighteenth-century zinc bath (complete with original taps) dominates the bathroom. The antique marble floor is heated from below, Roman-villa-style. Compared to the rest of the apartment, the bedroom is quite stark. Frédéric chose a bold black-and-white-striped fabric for the bedhead and valance, which plays up the white background perfectly.

3:2 RUSTIC RETREAT

One glance at Jorn Langberg's idyllic Suffolk cottage, with its traditional pink-washed walls and thatched roof, will make you green with envy. All is not what it seems, however, for inside the cottage there is an unusual blend of European influences unified by that most harmonious of all colours – grey. Jorn says he has always liked the colour: it gives out a cool feeling, which makes him feel very comfortable. In fact, grey has featured predominantly in both his private life and his career. 'I have lived in Denmark, Scotland and London, where you can always count on grey skies – much softer than blue,' he muses. 'I also worked for Christian Dior for twenty-five years and nowhere could be more synonymous with the colour grey than the House of Dior. From the packaging to the interior of the showrooms, everything was grey. No wonder I'm addicted to the colour!'

Jorn came to England from Denmark in 1952 to learn the language, but fell in love with the country and decided to stay. 'My father was very anxious I should continue my business studies but I had other ideas,' he recalls. To this end he enrolled at St Martin's College of Art, where he obtained his degree. He then went to work for Dior,. did his apprenticeship there, working his way up to become their chief designer in London. A few years later he was managing director.

During this time Jorn paid a visit to friends in East Anglia, where he came across a derelict early seventeenth-century cottage. 'It was a complete wreck but had enormous potential,' he recalls. The building originally belonged to the local farmer and was divided into three tiny cottages for the workers, so there were also three front doors, three sets of stairs and three inglenook fireplaces (the latter all in good working order). 'I bought a caravan, which I used as a weekend base while the work was carried out,' explains Jorn. 'It was rather cramped but great fun.' Over time the roof was rethatched, the floors lowered and the inside wall of a corridor taken down to create extra space and a better sense of proportion. He didn't use an architect but was lucky enough to meet a local builder sympathetic to old buildings, which made an enormous difference.

Today the exterior of the building resembles the quintessential country cottage, while inside the pace changes completely. Instead of traditional floral chintz and heavy oak furniture, there is a mixture of Scandinavian and English decoration – unified by the colour grey. Curiously ahead of his time, Jorn invested in painted furniture. Nobody was remotely interested in the stuff back then, he recalls. But being a designer means he is sensitive to changes – he knew it was the way forward.

In his own bedroom, bathroom and dressing room, for example, the beams and walls were limewashed, resulting in a delicious shade of pale grey, a complementary contrast to some of the other rooms with their unpainted beams and simple white walls. 'I was all set to use two different shades: a pale version for the walls and slightly darker tone for the beams,'

Jorn recalls. In the end a single colour was sufficient to provide a wonderful two-toned effect, as the dark wood of the beams filtered through. He painted the windows and the solid oak doors in a similar fashion. 'Pale colours can make small rooms appear lighter and larger than they really are, which is very helpful in old cottages,' he explains. 'You can always jolly the place up with something like a vase of red tulips. The odd splash of colour really stands out against a grey background.'

Downstairs a small hall connecting the drawing room and dining room is reminiscent of a cottage he once owned in Scotland – tartan rugs and paisley shawls combine with oak furniture and old leather chairs to play up the British appeal. This effect has also been applied to the drawing room (originally two rooms with a split-level floor), which is filled with handsome pale oak furniture and paved with the original floor bricks. The dining room, at the far end of the cottage, has a huge inglenook fireplace and a wealth of unpainted beams.

This is a house where entertaining regularly takes place, in a variety of different venues ranging from the dining room to the outside summer dining room to the garden room. The latter is a more recent addition, with large panes of glass sandwiched between old timber beams, soft pink walls and old oak floorboards. It's an indoor/outdoor room, and has a wonderful view of the garden.

But it's the 'studio' sitting room which really catches the eye. Floors limewashed in grey perfectly complement the colour of the walls and the Scandinavian woodburning stove, and both Louis XVI and Gustavian furniture look at home against the pale grey. Jorn explains that northern Swedish furniture was influenced by the French during the Napoleonic wars, but Danish furniture has a distinct German influence and is heavier, almost Baroque.

Twice a year the room is transformed into an art gallery to show off the work of contemporary British artists. 'When I left Dior I wanted to have something to do,' explains Jorn. 'As I had so many friends who were artists, I decided to put on an exhibition to show off their paintings. The first year went unbelievably well, the second was even better, and now, ten years later, we have more than doubled our turnover.' His latest project is *Art et Jardin*, where sculptors can exhibit their work alongside urns from Italy and pots from Burma as well as follies, aviaries, dovecotes and birdboxes. Jorn clearly enjoys every minute of the buildup, comparing it to the days of preparing for Dior collections. 'Everything has to be meticulous, as people visit from all over the country. It's also very rewarding to work alongside so many creative people and gives me enormous pleasure.'

ABOVE Jorn's latest project is *Art et Jardin* (Art and Garden), where sculptors can exhibit their work alongside urns from Italy or pots from Burma, or follies (such as this garden gate), aviaries, dovecotes and birdboxes.

OPPOSITE An old army trestle table is positioned along one wall in the studio/sitting room. A pair of Gustavian chairs flank the table, while a Louis XVI chair stands in the foreground. The painting sitting on the table is by Charles Williams.

LEFT & ABOVE In place of the traditional 'country cottage' floral chintz and heavy oak furniture, there is a mixture of Scandinavian and English decoration in the studio-cum-sitting-room – all unified by a grey colour theme. Floors limewashed in grey complement the colour of the walls and the woodburning fire to perfection. Being curiously ahead of his time, Jorn invested in painted furniture to decorate the cottage.

OPPOSITE & ABOVE Jorn painted the windows and solid oak doors in just one colour. He points out that pale colours make everything seem larger and brighter, which is very helpful in old cottages. An *Art et Jardin* zinc plinth, with eighteenth-century iron urn on top, can be seen through the double doors at the end of the building. The cottage has also been captured in a ceramic portrait by Jill Laurimore.

LEFT & OPPOSITE The beams and walls in the cottage's bedroom and bathroom were limewashed. This resulted in a delicious shade of pale grey – a complementary contrast to some of the other rooms in the cottage, with their unpainted beams and simple white walls. The bathroom houses a grey-painted Gustavian chair plus grey-upholstered footstool, which continues the cottage's colour theme, while an oak four-poster bed and ladder introduce some natural, unpainted wood into the bedroom.

OPPOSITE & ABOVE Jorn's garden is very controlled and architectural. Full of calm rooms in which one can sit alone and ponder, there are just a few flowers and no colours, with grey clapboard outbuildings, gravel and clipped hedges.

3:3 URBAN DISTINCTION

In 1996, David Gill purchased a disused handbag factory in Vauxhall, south London. 'I just had to have it,' he says. Not even the neighbouring tower blocks, gasometers or resident squatters could stand in his way after that, and he wanted the entire building, all 26,000 sq ft of it. 'I instinctively knew the building would make an amazing gallery'; indeed he is now the owner of 'the most surreal live/work space imaginable'. Over four years it was ingeniously transformed into an enormous complex, with offices and a roomy first-floor apartment. Always confident that art collectors from around the world would eke him out wherever he was based, he claims the location doesn't bother him, pointing out that his part of London is very up-and-coming, with the Tate Modern down the road, and Chelsea and the West End surprisingly close.

Born in Spain to a Spanish mother and a Franco-Dutch father, he spent most of his childhood in Barcelona. He came to London to study 'The Age of Baroque' at university, spent over four years at Christie's, then set up on his own. 'I became a serious collector in my teens, when I blew all my money on a small 1920s box,' he recalls. Today he has a remarkably tight grip on all that encompasses British taste – so much so that anyone looking for an insight into the aspirations of the next generation of urban sophisticates should seriously bear him in mind.

He opened a small, ultra-sophisticated gallery in London's Fulham Road in 1987. Specialising in furniture, fashion and design, he displayed classics by well-established designers from the 1930s to 1950s, alongside paintings by the New Romantics and jewellery by 1950s designer Line Vautrin. David also has a gift for spotting young talent – he was the first to represent contemporary artists such as Garouste & Bonetti, for example. The gallery swiftly became an important landmark in both fashionable and influential terms and his stable of young contemporaries proved just as important in today's world of design as they will be in the future. Collectors concentrated on 1930s to 1950s period pieces at the time, and it took a decade before they could embrace the new style of work as something inevitable and new, he explains. But David soon outgrew the gallery's limited space: 'Staging exhibitions ... meant taking everything out of the gallery to create enough room.'

Having bought the factory, David masterminded the building works with military precision. The factory has now been transformed into a a large gallery, and what was once a clutch of tiny offices now forms comfortable offices and spacious living quarters. The building was gutted, though great care was taken to ensure the basic architectural structure (the vast steel girders, the industrial windows, for example) remained in its original state, and that the character of the factory was retained. To introduce a sense of harmony within the new interior, he kept the architectural detailing exactly the same throughout the entire building and made sure each area and its various functions were interrelated. The rooms in his apartment have a similar feel to the gallery. 'I wanted space and versatility combined with open-plan living,' he recalls, and to achieve this he constructed three walls, around which he created a reception area, a bedroom with dressing and shower rooms, a kitchen and a small room that can be used as an office or occasional bedroom. Unsightly radiators are tucked away behind steel panels painted the same white colour as the walls. The windows, distressed in a subtle shade of industrial grey, are concealed behind simple white blinds that diffuse the light on bright, sunny days.

An expert on interiors, David tends to follow a certain style, architectural idea or period, but here he has successfully combined comfort and style with period and contemporary furniture and art work. 'I could easily have gone minimalist, with just a few paintings and one or two carefully selected pieces of minimal furniture, but I didn't feel it would give me the warmth I like in my own home.'

On entering the apartment visitors are ushered into a large L-shaped space housing the seating and dining areas; the entrance itself is separated from the rest of the room by 'The Love Slave Box', a curiously entitled cabinet designed by Richard Snyder. He says that when he works for a commission he creates a perfect situation where nothing is missing, but in his own home it's like a 'work in progress' – there's always the chance something new will turn up and need a home.

In the adjacent dining area, a gigantic bright-red painting by Abigail Lane takes centre stage on the wall. 'For me, furniture, paintings and objects are completely interrelated and no matter how passionate I may be about my latest acquisition, I have to find exactly the right place for it or it will seriously detract from the piece,' he explains.

David is constantly doing up houses for rock stars, supermodels and well-established collectors, then filling them up with things they like. 'I have a restless and inquiring mind that is either creating or on the lookout for what is happening today,' he says. 'My intuition allows me to recognise things as they are happening, or even before they happen, and to be able to say, 'Yes, this piece has great strength and will be a success.'

David now claims that the apartment is too small and has planning permission to convert a further 6000 sq ft at the top of the building into living accommodation. But it will take months of planning before he can begin, and will take at least a year and a half to complete once he starts. But is this out of necessity or passion – or both?

ABOVE & OPPOSITE A respected designer and collector of twentieth-century furniture, David Gill knew that the disused factory would make an amazing gallery. On the far side of the room the seating area is grouped around a magnificent steel and glass table. A splendid purple L-shaped sofa is the focus of the decoration ('I've had it for ever and I'll take it wherever I go,' he says).

ABOVE & RIGHT An extraordinary gilt-and-white-painted 1930s armchair, made by Emilio Terri for Charles Debestequi's Champs-Elysées apartment, sits in front of the simple metal console table that runs the length of an entire wall. The walls are painted white, but different shades of the same colour were incorporated in the scheme to create an impression of depth. The polished concrete floor, for instance, was given a decorative uplift with inset metal strips resembling a grid. The table in the dining area is made from two bronze plinths supporting an oval marble surface.

OPPOSITE, ABOVE & RIGHT   The rooms in the apartment – though smaller than the gallery – have a similar feel, with exposed beams, concrete floors and high ceilings. David's aim was to combine open-plan living with space and versatility, so he decided against doors, which he feels restrict freedom of movement. The matador painting, on the wall near the entrance, is by Aldo Mondino and a reference to David's half-Spanish nationality. The ceramic plate is one of a collection of Cocteau works in the apartment.

ABOVE & OPPOSITE Two narrow floor-to-ceiling openings in the walls link the sitting room, bathroom and bedroom, which contains this 1960s chair. Compared to the rest of the apartment, the purpose-built kitchen is definitely more masculine. it is very cool and clinical, with hard-edged surfaces and stainless-steel units. Access is via the only door in the flat, which leads from the dining area.

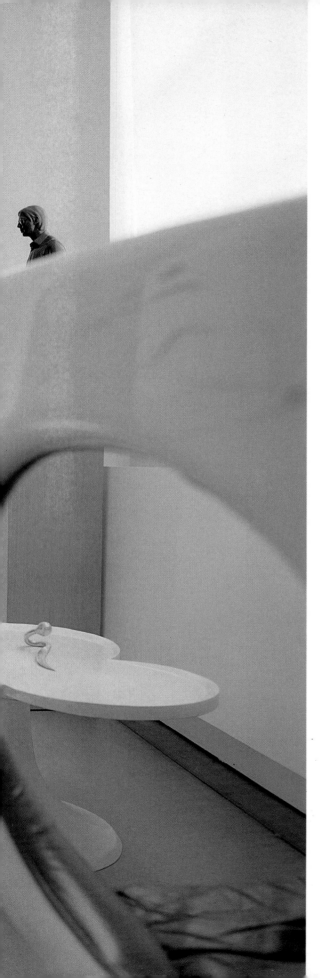

LEFT & ABOVE The main bedroom is dominated by a large leather double bed, which can be lit from below and behind so it appears to be floating. This relaxing effect was achieved by using thin striplights, butted tightly together to ensure there is no break in the lighting sequence. A compression painting by Mark Francis hangs alongside the bed, and a self-portrait by Don Brown stands on a wooden plinth in front of the window. The minimalist bathroom is a very personal place. It is the room David would rather not have to compromise on and where he likes to be completely alone. The column in the corner is by Elliniki.

3:4 EXQUISITE ALCHEMY

You would be hard pushed to sum up Hassan Abdullah's fabulously idiosyncratic home in a few neat phrases. And you wouldn't want to, either, because here is a bachelor pad that defies all the usual interior rules without a second thought. It's acid-bright, neo-Baroque, cutesy-kitsch and super-decadent all at once. It's theatre for the home, a stage set where Abdullah can mix and match his favourite eighteenth-century French antiques with 1960s psychedelia and flea-market gems – and get away with it. 'I don't aspire to be like anyone else or set out to impress,' says Malaysian-born Abdullah. 'I just want things around me that I love. I don't worry whether neighbours or friends will like it – it's really about myself.'

The flat is part of a converted Victorian pub in Shoreditch, London, and sits above the hip restaurant Les Trois Garçons that Abdullah set up, by way of accident really, with his two business partners. 'We threw a party with a cabaret theme and put up a stage and curtains,' he adds. 'It looked quite fun, so we decided to open a restaurant and give people what we expect ourselves – friendly service, fresh ingredients and great surroundings.' It's a recipe that has obviously worked, with A-list celebrities like Bianca Jagger, Nicole Kidman and Donatella Versace all queuing up for a table.

The top two floors of the four-storey building are now Abdullah's home, although it was completely derelict when he first moved in. 'Squatters had been living here for five years and taken out everything, including the heating pipes and radiators,' he recalls. 'It was like a war zone, but I could still see the spatial qualities of it.'

Today, with Abdullah's astute creative eye (he was an interior designer for a few years, but found it boringly formulaic), the flat has been transformed into a throbbing and magical festival of colours, furniture and textures that bombard every sense as soon as you step inside.

The huge double drawing room is a haphazard yet happy mix of ornate eighteenth- and nineteenth-century antiques – statues, chandeliers, tables, mirrors, even a pair of gold columns from a Russian palace – juxtaposed with an ultra-contemporary, vivid-purple, sweeping, hornlike chair. There is no theme as such; more just a love of beautiful things.

'I try to be open-minded and to look at each individual piece as an aesthetic form rather than how much it is worth,' explains Abdullah. 'People can become obsessed with collecting certain things, but for me it can be anything, like a little thimble or a wigstand. It is instinctive – when I see something beautiful, it shouts out to me, 'Here I am.'

Abdullah's shop Solaris on Notting Hill is a constant source of tempting pieces to bring home. Like his flat, it is a treasure trove of antique and modern furniture and artefacts from all periods (from the eighteenth century to the 1970s to the

OPPOSITE & ABOVE The huge double drawing room is a haphazard yet happy mix of ornate eighteenth- and nineteenth-century antiques (statues, chandeliers, tables, mirrors, even a pair of gold columns from a Russian palace) juxtaposed with an ultra-contemporary, vivd-purple sweeping hornlike chair. There is no theme as such – just a love of beautiful things.

present day) and attracts a star-studded clientele including Madonna and Yasmin Le Bon. 'When things come home from the shop I don't take them back,' smiles Abdullah. 'Sometimes I put a red 'Sold' sticker on a piece until I've made up my mind.' One such piece is the fabulous arched gilt headboard that started life in an eighteenth-century Italian church. It sits like a gilded halo above the vast bed in Abdullah's seductive midnight-blue bedroom with an original 1960s Verner Panton rug and elegant French 1920s dressing table for company. 'I wanted the bedroom to be cocooning, like an embryo,' muses Abdullah. 'Somewhere really cosy where you can drift away.'

It's not just Abdullah's finely tuned, pick-and-mix approach that makes the flat so unique, but his inventive way of using pieces in unexpected places. The rather grand bathroom panelling, for instance, is another architectural salvage-yard treasure that originally came from the inside of a lift in the Savoy Hotel, while an enormous pair of iron gates are used inside instead of doors. 'I like to divide things, but not solidly; otherwise it cuts the light and becomes a dead end,' adds Abdullah. 'And a gate entices you to go through and find out what's on the other side.' Here you'll find the chaotically bright TV room in a clash-happy mix of pillar-box red, fuchsia-pink and orange walls. 'I was inspired by YSL,' says Abdullah. 'I thought, 'If you can get away with these colours on clothes, why not with rooms?''

The colours are mixed in with 1960s and 1970s paraphernalia, including his beloved de Sede fawn kid-leather sofa which snakes around the room (originals can fetch up to £34,000 today) and light-up letters spelling out 'BABY' that once belonged in a fairground. There is also a series of mesmeric glass floating discs that act as a subtle room divider but look more like the hippest mobile you've ever seen.

It's not a place for children as Abdullah rightly admits, because there are so many valuable, breakable things at every turn. But that's not to say it's a precious, hands-off apartment. Far from it. Abdullah has parties aplenty, plus his two Dalmatians, Oscar and Max, are completely at ease in their Baroque, carnival surroundings. If you're wondering how the practicalities of a kitchen could ever fit into such a glorious madcap place, rest assured that there isn't one. That's to say, Abdullah treats the restaurant downstairs like an extension of his home. He eats there every night except Sunday, when he dines out.

'When people see my apartment they always say 'Wow, we want to live here. Can we stay?'' smiles Abdullah. 'Then they ask what possessed [me] to do it like this.'

But that's a question only Abdullah can answer.

RIGHT Today, with the help of Abdullah's astute creative eye, the flat has been transformed into a throbbing, magical festival of colours, furniture and textures that bombard every sense as soon as you step inside. An enormous pair of iron gates are used instead of a door, enticing you to go through and find out what's on the other side.

OPPOSITE & ABOVE The chaotically bright TV room – with its clash-happy mix of pillar-box red, fuchsia-pink and orange walls. The colours are mixed in with 1960s and 1970s paraphernalia, including Abdullah's beloved de Sede kid-leather sofa, which snakes around the room, and light-up letters spelling 'BABY' that came from a fairground. A series of mesmeric floating discs acts as a subtle room divider, but more resembles the hippest mobile you've ever seen.

ABOVE & OPPOSITE It is not just Abdullah's finely honed pick-and-mix approach that makes the flat

so unique, but also his inventive way of using pieces in unexpected places. The rather grand bathroom

panelling, for example, is an architectural salvage-yard treasure, and originally came from the inside of a

lift in the Savoy Hotel. Abdullah says his collecting is instinctive – when he sees something beautiful, it

shouts out to him, 'Here I am.'

PREVIOUS PAGE, OPPOSITE & ABOVE Abdullah's shop on Notting Hill is a constant source

of tempting pieces to bring home and, he says, 'When things come home from the shop I don't take

them back.' One such piece is the fabulous arched gilt headboard, which sits like a gilded halo

above the vast bed in his seductive midnight-blue bedroom. An original 1960s Verner Panton rug

and elegant French 1920s dressing table keep it company.

3:5 SCULPTED SOPHISTICATION

Antiques dealer Peter Hone has an ever-present twinkle in his eye – he exudes a heady concoction of education, eccentricity and wit guaranteed to spellbind the listener for hours. His career took off on a somewhat curious note, starting work as a chef for British Railways on the overnight trains from London to Scotland. He then graduated to hotels and was a top chef by the age of 18. When he realised eating *haute cuisine* was far more enjoyable than cooking it, he handed in his notice.

Very soon after, while browsing through the antique shops of London's Camden Passage, he came across a small shop for sale, which he bought for £200. He specialised in Regency furniture until prices became so high that he was forced to resort to larger, less expensive pieces. Two years later, at a house sale in Cornwall, Peter purchased a job lot of twenty-five four-poster beds – for £10 each. 'In no time I became known for my beds ... I sold [them] to all the pop stars of the time, including the Rolling Stones and the Beatles. It was enormous fun.' However, in 1979 the lure of architecture took a grip, and Peter gave up the shop to become a custodian for the Department of Environment's historic houses – issued with a bicycle and a kind of policeman's uniform with a truncheon and peaked hat with a silver crown on it, no less.

Peter's neighbour suggested a meeting with her brother, Lord Jacob Rothschild, who was looking for someone to run the antiques department of his latest venture, Clifton Nurseries, in west London. 'I thought, 'Oh dear me, no. I'm a civil servant now, I've signed the Official Secrets Act and I'm in line for a wage-related pension. Besides, I don't want to work for some high-powered person when I'm terribly happy cycling around London on my bike looking at beautiful houses,'' recalls Peter. Curiosity got the better of him, however, and a meeting was duly arranged. 'The moment we met I was completely won over,' says Peter with a wry smile. Ffifteen years later he remains an adviser to the company, although in essence he is his own boss. 'I spend most of my time looking for furniture and objects for clients. It's a marvellous life.'

As one might expect, Peter's own home is anything but conventional. On the first floor of a fine nineteenth-century stucco building overlooking communal gardens, the flat (which has no central heating) comprises one enormous high-ceilinged room, a tiny kitchen, a small hall and a bathroom and bedroom. When Peter first bought it, the flat had wall-to-wall carpeting and Regency striped wallpaper throughout. 'I ripped out the carpet to expose the old boards and displayed vast quantities of porcelain,' he explains. The following incarnation incorporated natural hessian walls and dark-green felt curtains. 'Monastic but wonderful,' Peter says. There then followed a chocolate-brown and stripped-pine phase, closely followed by a distinctly plush period with sumptuous red curtains originally made for Windsor Castle.

'My life completely changed the day I started working in the garden business,' maintains Peter. 'I became acutely aware that we are constantly surrounded by stone, which has been quarried by hand and worked on with love. Most of these pieces were once part of something very beautiful.'

The longer he worked for Clifton Nurseries, the more Peter became interested in stone. 'I spent all my free time reading, travelling and visiting important buildings,' he recalls. 'I was particularly drawn to Coade stone, an artificial stone manufactured in the eighteenth century and used for the architectural detailing on many great buildings, including Buckingham Palace and the Naval College at Greenwich.'

His first purchase was a stone lion, unearthed from the derelict garden of Thomas Hope's house in Surrey. 'Since then I've just collected and collected,' he admits. 'I know exactly where each fragment comes from and how I acquired it,' he says with evident pride. 'I like to think I'm preserving them for the nation!' For example, part of a plaster-cast frieze of the Parthenon, by Flaxman, was rescued from a house on Paddington Green. Passing the house on the bus one day, he saw that it was being demolished. 'Happily, the bulldozer had not yet attacked the plaques so I gave the workmen a fiver, hacked [them] off the wall, and took them home in a taxi.' It now hangs above the mantelpiece.

In the wonderfully proportioned sitting room, copies of nineteenth-century paper columns (discovered in the attic of a house in St Albans) flank the pair of doors leading into the hall and kitchen. A magnificent 1950s four-poster bed – a total snip, at £75 including curtains – takes centre stage in the winter months.

At the far end of the flat, the walls of the summer bedroom are painted green to match the colour of the early nineteenth-century chintz curtains rescued from imminent extinction on a bonfire. Above the bed is a picture of the Lake District by Edward Lear, discovered on top of a cupboard at a country-house sale and given to Peter by an unsuspecting porter.

Peter admits he cannot resist the lure of the hunt, of acquiring those one-off must-haves. 'I've picked up wonderful things for next to nothing and still continue to do so...I ferret around in the strangest of places and it's surprising what I turn up. However, if I find something really wonderful I'll go for it, irrespective of cost. I've just found an amazing set of plaster and wood pilasters, designed and made by Robert Adam fo Bowood House in Wiltshire after it was pulled down in 1962. Each section is a 12ft high and they are incredibly important – hopefully one of my clients will find a place for them. If not, I'll pop them on the ceiling!'

ABOVE & OPPOSITE The tiny hall connecting the sitting room and the bedroom is dominated by two magnificent plaster statues of Flora and Athene, one complete with sword and helmet. The entire apartment has been taken over by a vast array of stone objects and architectural fragments – 'My friends refer to my flat as the 'Hone Museum' because it looks like an extension of the John Soane Museum,' he says.

OPPOSITE & ABOVE The sitting room, with its wonderful proportions and the floor-to-ceiling windows leading onto a balcony running the full width of the property, is undeniably the heart of the apartment. Throughout the room, large quantities of friezes, rondels, plaques, swags, rosettes and architectural fragments are decoratively displayed on every conceivable surface and wall.

ABOVE & RIGHT Unbelievably, Peter knows exactly where each architectural fragment in his flat comes from – irrespective of its

size – and how he acquired it. He painted the walls the colour of stone, to provide a suitable backdrop for his pieces, and retained

the original scrubbed pine floor.

PREVIOUS PAGE, LEFT & ABOVE A magnificent four-poster bed takes centre stage in the main bedroom, but Peter admits

that the room gets so cold in winter that he moves it into the sitting room, where a comfortable seating area grouped round a

large round table is used as a workplace during the day and for dining at night. The summer bedroom has the aura of a

conservatory, with its double doors and small balcony. The walls have been painted a light green, enhanced by exquisite

antique white linen and woolwork bedspread. A collection of *bois dorée* plaques adorns the wall. Above the bed is a picture

of the Lake District by Edward Lear.

INDEX

ACKNOWLEDGMENTS

Grateful thanks to all the bachelors featured in Bachelor Style for letting us publish their homes. The book would
have been impossible without their cooperation and genuine enthusiasm for the project. I would also like to acknowledge
my editor Helen McFarland for her constant support, and Co & Bear for coming up with the initial concept for the book.

Contributing authors: Sally Griffiths (2002): Pp194-205. Pp168-179, Pp156-167, Pp146-155, Pp124-141, Pp102-123,
Pp90-101, Pp74-85, Pp44-53, Pp10-25, Lara Sargent(2002): Pp180-193, Judith Wilson(2002): Pp66-73,
Toby Alleyne-Gee(2002): Pp54-65, Abby Bussel /Interior Design.(2002): Pp36-43, Dominic Lutyens (2002): Pp26-35

Picture credits: © Ken Hayden(2002): p2, Pp194-205, Pp180-193, Pp168-179, Pp74-85, Pp10-25, p7 (**right**), p142
(**left**), p142 (**right**), p143 (**left**), © Andreas von Einseidel (2002): Pp156-167, Pp146-155, Pp102-123, p87 (**right**),
p143 (**right**), © Andrew Twort (2002): Pp124-141, Pp90-101, p86 (**left**), p86 (**right**), p87 (**left**), © Graham Atkins-Hughes
(2002): Pp66-73, p6 (**left**), © Reto Guntli (2002): Pp54-65, © James Merrell (2002): Pp44-53, © Michael Moran (2002):
Pp36-43, p7 (**left**), © Mark York (2002): Pp26-35, p6 (**right**).